THE
PRINT SHOP
IDEA
BOOK

Sherry Kinkoph

alpha
books

A Division of Prentice Hall Computer Publishing

11711 North College Avenue, Carmel, Indiana 46032 USA

To my sister, Melissa, and my crafty, creative friend, Shawn.

International Standard Book Number:1-56761-250-4
Library of Congress Catalog Card Number: 93-71187

95 94 93   8 7 6 5 4 3 2

Interpretation of the printing code: the rightmost number of the first series of numbers is the year of the book's printing; the rightmost number of the second series of numbers is the number of the book's printing. For example, a printing code of 93-1 shows that the first printing of the book occurred in 1993.

Screen reproductions in this book were created by means of the program Collage Plus from Inner Media, Inc., Hollis, NH.

Printed in the United States of America

Publisher

Marie Butler-Knight

Associate Publisher

Lisa A. Bucki

Managing Editor

Elizabeth Keaffaber

Development Editor

Seta Frantz

Manuscript Editor

Barry Childs-Helton

Cover Designer

Susan Kniola

Indexer

Craig Small

Production Team

Diana Bigham, Katy Bodenmiller, Brad Chinn, Scott Cook,
Tim Cox, Meshell Dinn, Mark Enochs, Howard Jones,
Tom Loveman, Carrie Roth, Beth Rago, Greg Simsic, Lillian Yates

Special thanks to C. Herbert Feltner for ensuring the technical accuracy of this book.

Contents

What Can You Do
with the Print Shop Programs?

Have you ever wanted to create your own greeting cards? Have you ever needed to make a poster or flyer for a sale or an upcoming event? Have you ever wanted to design your own banners to hang up at parties? The Print Shop programs can do all these things and more, right on your own computer. The Print Shop programs are for people tired of buying the same old generic stuff at the store. With the Print Shop programs, you can personalize, tailor-make, and design your own stationery, calendars, signs, advertising, useful computer crafts, and more.

This book will show you hundreds of ideas you can use around the home, office, or school. There are projects for families, professionals, and even projects just for kids. You'll learn how to make sale flyers, real estate signs, labels, newsletters, recipe cards, book markers, restaurant menus, and garage sale signs, to name just a few examples. If you have The New Print Shop or The Print Shop Deluxe on your computer, you can complete any of the project ideas in this book.

You'll also find special sections in this book covering the basics of getting in and out of the programs, showing you how to navigate the various menus, and providing tips for printing. You'll learn how to modify graphics, import your own art, and create your own special effects. At the end of the book are easy-to-look-up tables showing the available typestyles, and all the Print Shop Deluxe graphics. We sincerely believe you'll find this book to be the most comprehensive guide to the Print Shop programs.

At the very back of the book is a coupon to use to purchase additional Print Shop Deluxe Graphics Collections. These can increase your project potential by leaps and bounds!

Using a little imagination, combined with the power of your computer, you'll be amazed at the variety of creations available at your fingertips. But don't take our word for it—turn the page and find out for yourself.

Introduction

What You Need to Know about Print Shop

If you've never worked with the Print Shop programs before, this section will give you some important information for getting around in both The New Print Shop (DOS version) and The Print Shop Deluxe (DOS and Windows versions). If you're using Apple or Mac versions of the Print Shop programs, you'll find the ideas in this book can be easily adapted to your version of the program.

If you're already familiar with the Print Shop programs, you may want to skip ahead to the Projects section; there you'll find numerous ideas on how to use the Print Shop Programs, and step-by-step instructions for completing the projects.

Most of the instructions in this book will focus on the Print Shop Deluxe program (DOS and Windows), which is the latest version (including release 1.2). However, if you are using The New Print Shop, you'll find plenty of guidance—and special tips for completing the projects using your program's capabilities.

If you're a new computer user, you may encounter terms you're not familiar with. If they are not immediately defined, please look at the definitions at the end of this section for help.

About the Programs

The original Print Shop, created by Broderbund Software in 1984, was a phenomenally popular program among adults and children. Just as the name implies, the program allowed you to create all kinds of materials normally associated with a printing company. Best of all, it was incredibly easy, and turned your computer into a virtual stationery store. In 1989, Broderbund updated this program as The New Print Shop (NPS), an improved version with higher-resolution graphics, more flexibility, and better printing quality. The popular program became even easier to use. Broderbund also created add-on pieces that further the program's capabilities. There are Graphics Libraries (such as the Sampler Edition, the Party Edition, the School and Business Edition) that provide more art to use. The New Print Shop Companion add-on lets you create flyers, envelopes, and newsletters.

In 1992, Broderbund introduced The Print Shop Deluxe (PSD), with an improved graphical interface that featured even greater flexibility. In PSD, scalable graphics are introduced—crisper and in full color, there are more detailed layouts for each project type, and scalable fonts and special effects make the design potential almost limitless. Broderbund has also created several PSD Graphics Collections that feature more art: Business Graphics, Sampler Graphics, Comic Characters, Amazing Animals, Celebrations, Sports Graphics—among others, and there are sure to be more to come!

The latest release of PSD, 1.2, allows you to import and export graphics from other programs, as well as adding some more options to the already great features.

DOS and Windows? If you're new to the world of computers, running across the terms *DOS* and *Windows* may throw you for a loop. But don't panic, they're easily explained. DOS stands for *Disk Operating System*, a program that provides the most basic instructions your computer needs to operate. DOS is the "boss" of your computer system. It organizes, interprets, and carries out your every command.

Windows is a program that runs on top of your computer's DOS system, and gives everything a friendly, visual approach. It dresses up DOS and makes it look less intimidating. Windows is a *graphical user interface* that lets you choose commands by using menus or icons. (*Icons* are little pictures.)

What's the Difference?

You may be wondering what differences exist between The New Print Shop and the latest version, The Print Shop Deluxe. The major difference is technology. The newer deluxe program takes advantage of the newest technological advances in computers (386 and 486 microprocessors, VGA and Super VGA display adapters, and hard drives). But to most users, what's going on inside a computer isn't as interesting as what appears on-screen. So for the rest of us non-technically-oriented people, the primary difference between the programs is appearance. Take a look at Figure 1.1 to see how the older NPS screen looks. NPS has plainer-looking screens, and up until version 3.3, was for the most part, monochrome (black and white). Now look at

Figure 1.2 to see what a PSD screen looks like. The deluxe version offers full-color screens that have a polished, design-oriented look.

Figure 1.1
Intro screen from
The New Print Shop.

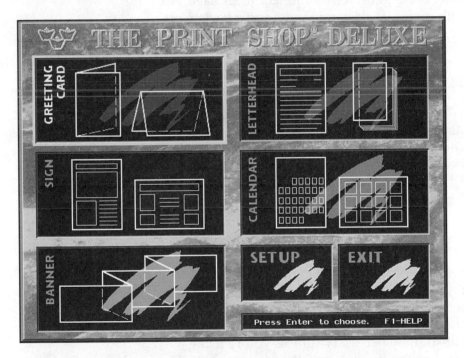

Figure 1.2
Intro screen from
The Print Shop
Deluxe, DOS
version.

Fonts and graphics make up another difference between the programs. NPS has 12 fonts or typefaces available, and numerous graphics selections. NPS fonts and graphics are not scalable and will print with jaggies, or jagged edges when you look up close. PSD for both DOS and Windows offers 30 fonts and hundreds of graphics, all of which are scalable and print without jaggies. (If you're using Windows 3.1, TrueType fonts are also available.) Its newer technology also allows an improvement in graphics; PSD offers more graphics of varying types, and even wider flexibility if you want to modify them within the program.

PSD release 1.2 has undergone a few changes from the first version. It's now faster at drawing your projects on-screen and it's faster at printing them. You can now import graphics from other programs with similar file formats and export PSD graphics as well. Banners print more smoothly, the calendar projects can now be scaled, and the program supports four new languages: French, German, Spanish, and Italian. Also, with the vast variety of printers available from various manufacturers, release 1.2 has added more printer support.

Aside from these differences in programs, you can still create the same great projects, ranging from stationery to signage. All are easy to use, with menu-based commands, and a variety of graphics.

The original Print Shop for the Mac uses a similar approach as found in IBM versions of the program. Projects are created through a series of menu steps. However, the Mac version utilizes the familiar Macintosh screen format and user-friendly appeal. In addition, Mac users can import drawings from MacPaint and the clipboard, use the Graphic Editor to change existing art, and add new fonts. In 1993, Broderbund plans to release a Mac version of its PSD program.

What Do You Need to Get Started?

Other than a creative spirit, the first tangible item you need to get started is a copy of NPS or PSD up and running on your computer. The second thing you need is a printer to print out your projects. A mouse is very nice, especially with the Deluxe program, but not absolutely necessary (unless you're using PSD-Windows). Aside from these things, there's not much else to worry about.

Installation Help   Have you installed one of these programs on your computer? See the installation appendix at the back of this book for instructions and help.

To start your Print Shop program:

The New Print Shop/DOS

1.   Change to the drive and directory where you installed the program. For example, if the program is on your hard drive, this will probably be **C:\NEWPS>**.

2.   Type **PS**, then press Enter.

Print Shop Deluxe/DOS

1.   Change to the drive and directory where you installed the program. For example, if the program is on your hard drive, this will probably be **C:\PSDELUXE>**.

2.   Type **PSD**, then press Enter.

Print Shop Deluxe/Windows

1.   From the Windows Program Manager screen, double-click on the Program Group icon.

2.   Double-click on the Print Shop Deluxe icon.

(What's a double-click? Don't worry. It's part of using the mouse, and we'll show you how to do it later in this section.)

What's on Your Screen?

The first screen you see after starting your program is called the *Main menu* screen. This is where all of your projects start. This is also where you exit the program. Figure 1.3 shows the Main menu screen from PSD-DOS version. The *Title bar*, showing the name of the program, is incorporated into the design of the startup screen. Below the Title bar are *menu selections* that look like large buttons. In the bottom corner is an *Info box* that offers you some directions in case you forget what to do.

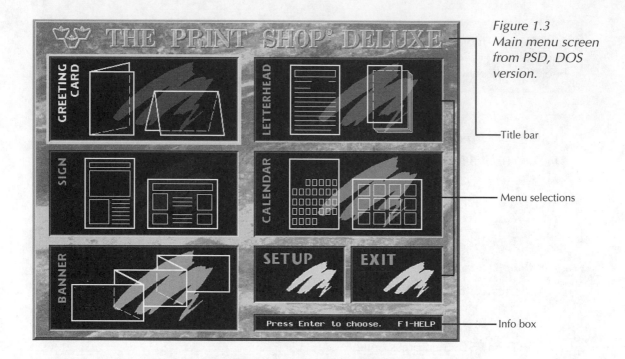

Figure 1.3
Main menu screen
from PSD, DOS
version.

Title bar

Menu selections

Info box

Figure 1.4 shows how that same screen looks in the PSD-Windows version. The startup screen in Windows does not take up a full screen. Instead it is more of a "window" within the screen. Again, you'll find a Title bar and menu selections. The selections on this screen also look like large buttons. The *Control menu box* lets you change the size of your window, close the window, or switch to another window. If you're already familiar with Windows, you'll find the same old Windows controls available in this version of PSD. If you're a new Windows user, look for tips and special instructions to help you along the way.

Figure 1.5 shows the Main menu from NPS. This version shows both a *menu* listing with the project selections, and a *Preview window* that shows a picture (in open area to the right of your screen) of what the project looks like. In addition, there is an Info box with information about what keys to press, as well as a *Message area* that gives you further directions on how to proceed.

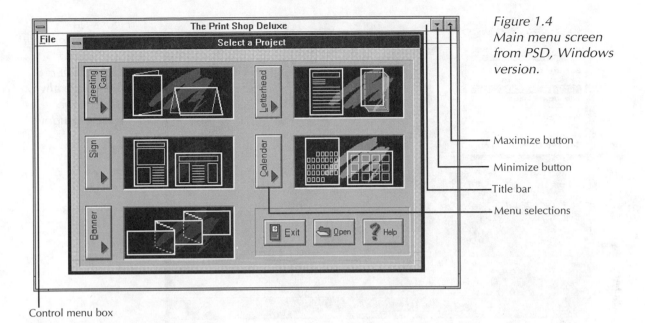

Figure 1.4
Main menu screen
from PSD, Windows
version.

Maximize button

Minimize button

Title bar

Menu selections

Control menu box

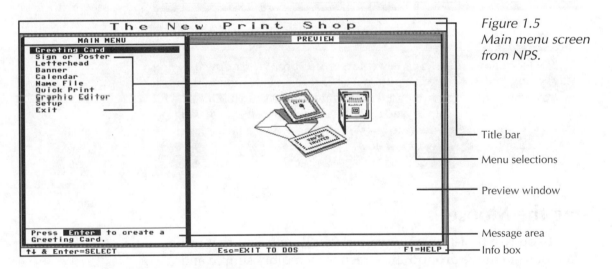

Figure 1.5
Main menu screen
from NPS.

Title bar

Menu selections

Preview window

Message area

Info box

Once you've started a project, you'll always be able to see how it looks in the Preview window (not to be confused with the Preview command, which you'll learn more about in this section). Figure 1.6 shows an example of a project shown on the Preview window of PSD-DOS version.

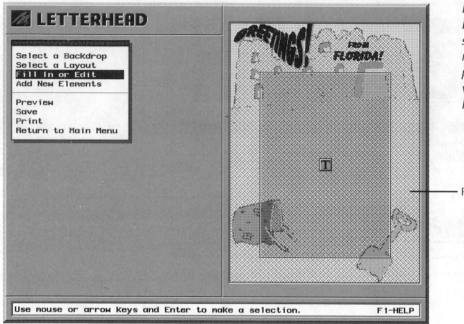

Figure 1.6
Regardless of what
stage you've
reached, your
projects are always
visible in the
Preview window.

Preview window

PSD-Windows Tip   You can enlarge your project window by clicking on the Maximize button (see Figure 1.4), the box with an arrow pointing up, in the top right corner of the screen. This enlarges your working window to fill the whole screen. Clicking on the Minimize arrow (the box with the downward arrow) will decrease the size of your window.

Using the Mouse

If you're a first-time mouse user, you'll soon find that using a mouse to move around the screen is incredibly simple and intuitive. First of all, place your right hand over the mouse, and your index finger over the left mouse button. (Lefties will have to do the opposite.) To move the mouse, gently push it around on your desktop. As you do, you'll notice something happening on your screen. If you're using NPS or PSD-DOS version, a *highlight bar* or *box* moves around on the screen as you move your mouse around on the desk. If you're using PSD-Windows version, you'll notice an arrow, called a *mouse pointer*, that moves on the screen whenever you move your mouse.

Regardless of whether you see a highlight bar or a pointer, the effect is the same—you're moving around the screen.

When you want to make a selection using the mouse, simply move the highlight bar onto the selection (or point the arrow at it), then click the left mouse button. A *click* is a quick tap or press of the mouse button. Some selections require a *double-click*, two quick taps of the mouse button. To move an object on your screen to a new position, you must drag it with the mouse. *Dragging* is pointing to the object, holding down the mouse button, and moving the mouse. When the new position is reached, let go of the mouse button. That's all there is to using the mouse.

> *Mouse Note* If you're using PSD-DOS version, you will find uses for both the left and right mouse buttons in the program. Pressed simultaneously, they act like the **Tab** key; they take you to different sections of the menu. Clicking the right mouse button is the same as pressing **Esc**, which takes you back a step in your project. If you're using NPS, you'll find that the right mouse button works like an Esc key in just the same way.

Using the Keyboard

If you're more comfortable using the keyboard rather than a mouse, you'll be happy to know that it's quite effortless to move around your screen using the arrow keys on the keyboard. When your selection becomes *highlighted* (or surrounded by a black box), just press the Enter key.

Aside from the **arrow** keys, you'll also find yourself using the **Esc** key to go backward a step in your project. If you're using NPS, you'll also be pressing the F-Keys, or the *function keys*, to edit your text. In such cases, the menu box or the Info box will tell you how to use these keys.

You'll also find selection keys to use with the Alt key. *Selection keys* are shortcuts on the keyboard that correspond to menus on the screen. Selection keys are usually bold or underlined when they appear in a menu. For example, in Figure 1.6, the word *Save* in the menu box in the upper left of the screen has a bold, colored S. Rather than moving the keyboard arrows or the mouse to select the word "Save," you hold down the Alt key and press the letter S on the keyboard. This simple step accomplishes the same thing as using the arrow keys or mouse! Look for these keyboard selection letter keys throughout your program. We've also marked them in the project section of this book.

There are steps within the projects that require typing in text from the keyboard. When you reach such a place, the highlight bar or arrow becomes a blinking line or bar called a *cursor*. A cursor always indicates where to type the next letter. When typing is complete, you're back to moving around with the mouse or arrow keys.

Keyboard Tips These keys on the keyboard move the *highlight bar* (that black bar that appears over menu items when you want to choose them) around the screen.

↑ (Up arrow)	Moves up one item on a list.
↓ (Down arrow)	Moves down one item on a list.
Home	Takes you to the beginning of the list.
End	Takes you to the end of the list.
PgUp	Moves up one screen.
PgDn	Moves down one screen.

Note: These keys won't work if Num Lock is in effect.

How the Program Works

Although the screens differ slightly from one program to the next, the basic procedures are the same. You pick a project type, design it, and print it out. All of this happens through a variety of menus and dialog boxes.

You can assemble each project by using a series of menus and dialog boxes to choose borders and artwork, and type in text. Along the way, you can customize, experiment, and preview your work. At any point, you can stop and *edit* (or change) your project. Each project can be saved and used again and again. Unlike other intimidating software programs available, the Print Shop programs really are quite foolproof.

For example, here's a sequence of menus used to create a simple letterhead using PSD-DOS version. Follow along with the captions to see how each step progresses. You'll be amazed at how easy it is to create a project.

1. First select a project type from the Main menu screen. For this example, choose Letterhead.

2. Next, select a new letterhead project.

3. Select letterhead orientation. For this example, choose a regular full-page orientation.

4. From the next menu that appears, you can start building your letterhead by choosing Select a Backdrop. (Not available on NPS.)

5. A backdrop dialog box appears next, from which you can choose a particular graphic design. Each design on the list can be viewed at the left of the dialog box before you make a selection. "Try it before you buy it!"

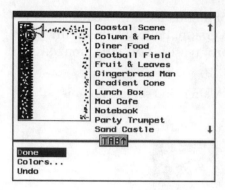

6. The next step is to pick out a layout for the letterhead. Choose Select a Layout from the menu list.

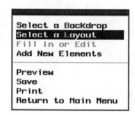

7. Choose a specific layout design to complement your letterhead graphic. (You'll learn more about layouts in the pages ahead.)

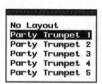

8. After you've picked a layout, you're ready to fill it in. Choose Fill In or Edit from the menu list.

9. After you choose the particular text block you want to fill in, a text dialog box will appear. Here you can type in the text, choose styles, sizes, positioning, and more.

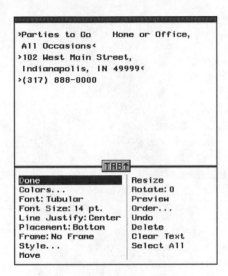

10. Once the letterhead is finished, and every part of the layout filled in, you're ready to print the project out on your printer. Choose Print from the menu list.

11. Here's what the finished letterhead looks like.

All versions of the Print Shop programs follow similar menu sequences. They will look different, depending upon what program and version you have, but the idea is the same—to piece together a project, step by step, using menus and dialog boxes.

If you use NPS or PSD-Windows version, here are some differences you will encounter in the same letterhead project sequence.

NPS: The screens in steps 1–2 will look markedly different in your program, but the selections are the same as the examples shown. Steps 3–9 are in a different sequence. Like the PSD users, you also choose steps from a menu list, but your list is in a different order. Instead of choosing a backdrop, you would choose Graphic from the menu list. Two menu screens follow that allow you to pick a layout and a particular piece of art to use. And just like the PSD example, you can preview how the design looks before actually choosing it. After a graphic is chosen, you then choose Text from the menu list. The next three menus allow you to choose a particular font, style, and type in the text. Once these steps have been completed, your project is ready to print!

Every time you complete a part of a project (such as typing the message in a greeting card), a checkmark appears by the menu item. This will help you keep track of project parts you've completed.

PSD-Windows: Steps 1–3 are pretty much the same in PSD-Windows as they are in DOS. There's only a slight difference in the appearance of the screens. However, rather than lead you through menu lists to complete your project in steps 4–9, the Windows version offers you dialog boxes to choose a backdrop and layout, and to fill in text. Once you've selected a layout, your screen will widen into a regular Windows program screen, and you'll have access to a menu bar and a Tool Palette. You'll learn how to use these as you read this section.

Menus and Dialog Boxes

Menus and dialog boxes are the key to getting around in the Print Shop programs. The menus and dialog boxes used in the Print Shop programs are very straightforward and easy to use. If at any time you forget what to do, an Info box at the bottom of the screen reminds you how to proceed (except in PSD-Windows). Windows users can use the Help option in times of trouble.

If you're using Print Shop for the Mac, you'll find menus and dialog boxes similar to those described for PSD-Windows. The menu bar and its subsequent drop-down menus are used to make common selections for any project type, such as print.

Using Menus

Menus are special boxes that allow you to make choices regarding steps, designs, layouts, and more. A menu in the Print Shop programs usually appears as a list of things you can do. Take a look at the menu list shown in Figure 1.7.

*Figure 1.7
Menu list from
PSD-DOS version.*

To choose a menu item, you must highlight your selection using the mouse or the keyboard. (*Highlighting* causes a black bar to appear over the selection, and the words become white.) To use the mouse, move the highlight bar or mouse pointer to the menu item, and click the left mouse button. To use the keyboard, use the arrow keys to move the pointer to the desired selection, then press Enter.

Many menu lists are too long to fit everything on one screen. In these cases, you'll notice a *scroll bar* on the menu, with arrows on either end. When you see arrows like these, this means there's more of the menu list to look at. Figure 1.8 shows an example of this type of menu. To scroll through a list, move your mouse pointer to the top or bottom (depending on which direction you want to scroll), or use the arrows on your keyboard.

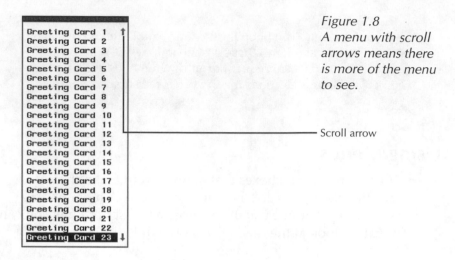

Figure 1.8
A menu with scroll arrows means there is more of the menu to see.

Scroll arrow

If you're using PSD-DOS version, you'll encounter yet another kind of menu containing two sections. In between the two sections is a Tab button. The top section contains a menu list. After choosing an item from the menu list, you can tab to the bottom section to continue your selections. Figure 1.9 shows an example of this kind of menu.

Mouse Note If you're using PSD-DOS version, you can hold down both mouse buttons to tab between the two menu sections.

Figure 1.9
A menu with two sections containing selections to be made, PSD-DOS version, release 1.2.

Menu Tip Any time you see menu items shaded in gray, that means they are not able to function for that particular task. In other words, they are not available or turned on. Attempts to select shaded menu items will be in vain.

Using Dialog Boxes

Dialog boxes are special boxes that give you more information about a particular command or require you to input more information before the command can be carried out. You can use your mouse to point at parts of the box and then click, or use the arrow keys on your keyboard to move around the dialog box and make selections. You can also use selection keys. Figure 1.10 shows an example of a dialog box from the PSD-Windows version.

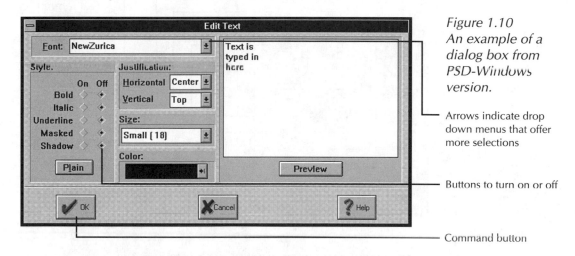

*Figure 1.10
An example of a dialog box from PSD-Windows version.*

Arrows indicate drop down menus that offer more selections

Buttons to turn on or off

Command button

Most dialog boxes want you to type something in or turn something on. The dialog box shown in Figure 1.10 is no exception. If you're using PSD-Windows, this particular dialog box appears when you're ready to fill in or edit a text block. (You'll learn about text blocks later.) There's a space for typing in text, drop-down menus from which to choose fonts and alignment, and option buttons you can use to turn on bold, italic, and other special treatments for your text. To exit the box, select OK or cancel.

Building Blocks and Layouts

Print Shop projects are assembled with several elements. These elements often look like blocks on your screen. There are borders, graphic blocks, ruled line blocks, text blocks, and headline blocks. These elements can be combined hundreds of different ways. The various elements appear as gray shaded boxes on your screen until you fill each one. These elements together make up your layout.

A *layout* provides designated areas for each element of your project. It's kind of like having a map of where each part goes. All you have to do is plug in text, graphics, headlines, and borders in the places the layout designates they should go. Figure 1.11 shows a sample layout from PSD-DOS version. Layouts always appear in the Preview window of your screen.

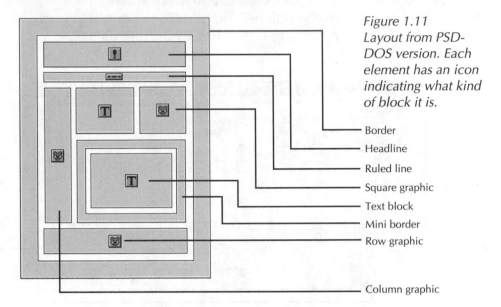

Figure 1.11 Layout from PSD-DOS version. Each element has an icon indicating what kind of block it is.

Border
Headline
Ruled line
Square graphic
Text block
Mini border
Row graphic

Column graphic

The Print Shop programs have been created with lots of layouts for each project type. You also have the option of designing your own layout. At any point in your project, you can modify or completely change the layout you have chosen. When you're finished with a project, you can always go back and edit the various elements.

If you're using PSD, you'll notice special icons, or little pictures, in the center of elements. (See Figure 1.11.)

- A tiny square with the letter T indicates that element is a *text block*. You'll be typing in text to appear in this block.

- A tiny square with an exclamation mark (!) indicates a *headline block*. This is where you'll type in a headline for your project.

- A tiny square with a picture of a bear indicates a *graphic*. Depending upon your layout, the graphic can be a *square graphic*, a *row graphic*, or a *column graphic*. These graphic blocks are where you'll select art to appear in your project.

- A tiny rectangle with dotted lines indicates a *ruled line block*. This element is for placing lines of varying thickness in your layout.

The border elements do not use icons because they are readily identified as looking like gray shaded frames within your project. Miniature *borders* are used around text blocks and graphics.

If you're using NPS, you will not find icons indicating element types in your program. Graphics are handled more simply. When you work on a project, the NPS menus will take you through the process of selecting borders, graphics, and text, one element at a time. Once the elements are chosen, they can always be customized or changed.

> If you're working with The Print Shop for the Mac, you'll find yourself assembling your project one element at a time, not unlike NPS users.

To choose an element to fill in or edit, highlight it by moving your mouse over the block until a box appears around the element. Select the element by clicking the mouse button. (Windows users should double-click the mouse button.) If you're using the keyboard, highlight the block with the arrow keys and press Enter.

Menus will appear, directing you how to proceed. Once you've chosen an element, you can unchoose it at any time by pressing Esc.

More About Graphic Elements

PSD (DOS and Windows) offers three types of graphic shapes to work with: square, row, or column (see Figure 1.11). *Square graphics* fit inside a square shape. *Row graphics* are elongated to fit inside a horizontal shape. *Column graphics* are just the opposite of row graphics (elongated to fit into vertical shapes).

As if this were not enough to choose from, you can also choose from a variety of design options to change a graphic. Adding shadows and frames, rotating, flipping, moving, scaling, and stretching are all ways to edit your graphic selection.

You can change a graphic through a menu that allows you to make edits. Figure 1.12 shows an editing menu from PSD-DOS version.

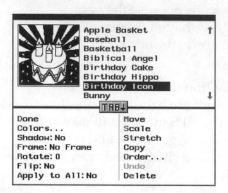

Figure 1.12 Graphics editing menu from PSD-DOS version.

If you're using NPS, your editing menu (called a *Customize menu*) offers options similar to those found in the PSD-DOS program. If you're using PSD-Windows, you'll find a slightly different approach for editing graphics. Instead of an editing menu, there is a handy-dandy *Tool Palette* (pictured in Figure 1.13), that has icons for quick editing at a click of the mouse button.

PSD-Windows Tool Palette

The Tool Palette has eight tools and a Color Control Panel. Take a look at Figure 1.13.

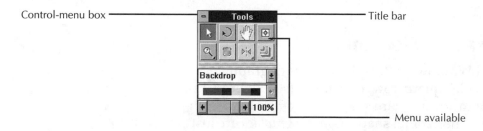

Figure 1.13 PSD-Windows version has a Tool Palette to help edit graphics elements in a project.

You can select a tool by clicking on it. Some tools have a tiny triangle in the lower right corner. This indicates there's a menu to see. To reveal the menu, move the pointer to the tool and hold down the mouse button. (These menus are also available from the Menu bar at the top of the window.)

You can drag your Tool Palette to another area of the screen by pointing at the Drag bar (or title bar), holding down the mouse button, and moving the mouse. You can also close the Tool Palette by double-clicking the Close box (or control menu box) or by selecting Hide Tools from the View menu on the Menu bar. To return the palette to your screen, select Show Tools from the View menu.

Here's a list of the palette tools and what they do:

The *Pointer tool* (the mouse pointer arrow) lets you select the different elements in your layout. It also helps with resizing and moving elements around.

The *New Object tool* is used to add new elements to your layout, such as text blocks, square graphics, or borders.

The *Hand tool* allows you to move your project around inside the window.

The *Zoom tool* changes the way your project is displayed. To get a close up, zoom in. To get a wide view, zoom out. There are also specific zoom sizes to select.

The *Delete tool* does exactly that—it deletes whatever is highlighted on your layout.

The *Rotate tool* allows you to tilt and turn an element in your layout.

The *Flip tool* lets you flip an element horizontally, vertically, or both.

The *Frame tool* is used for placing borders around elements in your layout.

The *Color Control panel* allows you to choose specific colors for parts of your layout.

When you first try out the Print Shop programs, experiment with the different design options to see how they work. You'll find a section detailing more about graphics later on in this book.

More About Text Elements

Just as with the graphics elements, text and headline blocks also offer you greater flexibility in designing your projects (though this is true for PSD users more than for NPS users). Not only can you select from a variety of typestyles, but you can also work with different sizes, colors, placement, and more.

Text can be modified letter by letter, word by word, sentence by sentence, or all at once. Text blocks can be resized, rotated, or moved. Fonts are often available in different styles, such as italic or bold. Headline text can take all sorts of shapes. When it comes to text, you'll find many different possibilities with the

Print Shop programs. We've included a font table at the back of this book that will show you what's available. (If you're using NPS, your program does not have headline blocks. However, text blocks can easily be used to create headlines.)

To choose a text block to fill in or edit:

1. Highlight the text block by moving the mouse pointer to the block you wish to select (or pressing the arrow keys until it's highlighted). When an element in your layout is highlighted, a box appears around the element.

2. Select the element by clicking the mouse button. (Windows users should double-click the mouse button.) If you're using the keyboard, highlight the block with the arrow keys and press Enter.

Menus will appear directing you how to proceed with the edit. Once you've chosen an element, you can unchoose it at any time by pressing Esc (or Cancel in PSD-Windows).

Preview Your Project

It's especially nice to be able to preview your project as a final check before you print it out, or just to see how it's progressing. The Preview function of the Print Shop programs is a valuable feature to use during any step of the project. Earlier in this section, you learned that within all of the Print Shop programs, there is a preview area at the right of your screen that illustrates your progress during each step. With some projects, however, you might want a bigger overall view of the project, or perhaps you would like to see what it looks like in color. With PSD, you have expanded preview options.

Figure 1.14 shows a PSD preview menu. In both the DOS and Windows versions you may choose three preview options: Color, Black and White, or Coloring Book. If you're using PSD-DOS, you can select Preview from the menu list. If you're using PSD-Windows, you must first pull down the **View** menu, then select Preview.

Figure 1.14
Preview options
available on PSD.

When you select Color Preview, the screen will display a larger image of your project in color. (You'll need a color monitor to see it in color, of course.) If your project is too big to be viewed in its entirety on one screen (a banner, for example), use the plus (+) or minus (–) keys to scroll along and view.

When you select Black & White Preview, the screen will display a monochrome image of your project. If you choose Coloring Book Preview, the screen will display your project in outline form, similar to a child's coloring book. You can later print out your project in Coloring Book style. Figure 1.15 shows an example of the Coloring Book preview option from PSD-DOS.

Figure 1.15 PSD-DOS version preview screen showing the Coloring Book preview option.

Press Esc or select Done to stop the preview at any time.

If you're using Print Shop for the Mac, you'll find a Preview option on the selection menu that works similarly to the Preview option described for PSD users.

What About Files?

After you've finished a project and previewed it, you're ready to save it and turn it into a file, assuming you plan to use it again. *Files* are created whenever you save a project you've made. Each file you create should be given a unique name to distinguish it from other files. Within a file is information pertaining to your project, whether it be a small greeting card or a large banner.

The Print Shop programs offer several different ways to save a file, depending on which program version you have. If you are using NPS or PSD, you can save a file on your hard disk drive, and also onto a floppy disk.

If you are using PSD you can use a *Full Save* or a *Quick/Fast Save*. (In PSD-DOS, it's called a *Quick Save*. In PSD-Windows, it's called a *Fast Save*.) What's the difference? A Full Save includes all graphics. A Quick Save just *references* the graphics. In other words, it codes the file with information on where to pick up those graphics (kind of like an ID number). A Full Save is handy when you want to give your file to another Print Shop user who doesn't have all the graphics you used in your project. A Full Save stores the complete project intact. However, a Full Save takes up a lot more room on your disk. Most of the time, Quick Save is the best way to save a file. But you'll want to keep in mind how your project will be used in the future—and how much room you have on your disk—when you make these choices.

Saving a File

To save a file when you have completed a project:

1.   Select Save from the menu list. (Windows users will have to pull down the File menu to choose Save.)

2.   When prompted, type in the name you wish to give your project (eight-character maximum). Additionally, you may add a description of your project where indicated. A description may help you identify the project later on.

To see how a file name is entered, look at Figure 1.16.

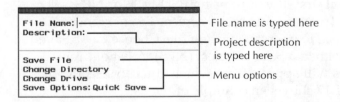

*Figure 1.16
The file name is typed in this dialog box from PSD-DOS version.*

Save to Floppies To save a file to a floppy disk, first make sure a disk is in the appropriate disk drive. After choosing Save from the menu list, follow the procedures for your Print Shop program version.

PSD-DOS:

1. Type in the file name (and description if desired).

2. Select Change Drive.

3. Select the drive containing your floppy disk.

4. Select Save File.

PSD-Windows:

1. Double-click on the drive letter from the directory list.

2. Type in the file name in the Filename box.

3. Click on OK or press Enter.

NPS:

1. Type in the file name.

2. Press the F9 key.

3. Select the drive letter containing your floppy disk.

4. Press Enter to save.

PSD-Windows Tip Use Save As from the File menu to save a previously saved project under a new file name. For example, you could save a greeting card with the same graphic but different text.

Using an Existing File

To work on a file you've created and saved before, you'll need to retrieve it first. If you're using PSD-DOS or NPS, select the project type from the first menu screen. The next menu gives you a chance to open an existing file. Choose Get a Saved Project (PSD) or Load a Saved Project (NPS). A list of previously saved files will appear, from which you can select your project. Figure 1.17 shows an example of file list.

If you're using PSD-Windows, you can select the **O**pen button on the Main menu screen. A dialog box will appear with a list of previously saved files. Highlight the project you want, and press Enter or click on OK.

PSD-Windows Tip   If you don't see the file you're looking for, make sure the correct project type is selected.

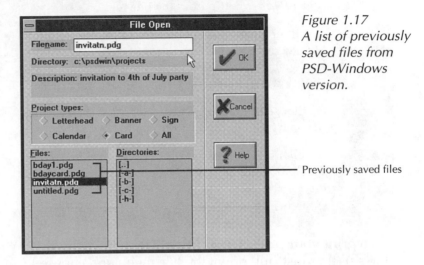

Figure 1.17
A list of previously saved files from PSD-Windows version.

Previously saved files

Printing

The last thing to do when you've completed a project is print it out. Before you begin the steps to printing out a project, it will be beneficial to set up your printer first.

How to Set Up your Printer

PSD-DOS and NPS:

1. Select Setup from the Main menu screen.

2. Depending upon your printer make and model, and how you have it hooked up to your computer, enter in the correct information where needed.

Select Printer requires you to identify the printer model you are using. Select Printer Port is where you identify which port your printer is hooked up to. Usually this is LPT1. Test Printer, when

continues

continued

selected, will run a test of whether your printer and port settings are correct. If everything is correct, a message will print out: **Welcome to The Print Shop** or **Welcome to The Print Shop Deluxe**. If no message prints out during your Test Printer test, check each setting again, and consult your printer manual.

PSD-Windows:

1. Select Printer Setup from the File menu.

2. A Printer Setup dialog box appears, showing the current list of printer drivers available (the list is based on what you specified when you installed your Windows program).

3. To choose further Windows printing options, select **S**etup from the Printer Setup dialog box.

4. Another dialog box appears. All the options in this dialog box are controlled by the Windows program, and not by PSD. If you need help with the other options, consult your Windows manual.

To print your project, select Print from the menu list. (Windows users must pull down the **F**ile menu and choose P**r**int.) A menu like the one shown in Figure 1.18 will appear, offering you printing options (such as Number of Copies). After making any other appropriate selections, choose Print, and the printer will be off and running.

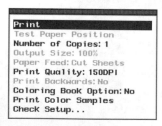

*Figure 1.18
Print menu options
from PSD-DOS
version.*

Because of the different size and scope of the projects you create with the Print Shop programs, there are several options to printing. For example, both PSD and NPS users can control the size of the printed project, whether it be a tiny gift enclosure card or an extra-large sign. Here are brief explanations and steps to using these other printing options.

Test Paper Position lets you position the paper in the printer so that it prints out at the correct place. (This test isn't useful for laser printers or sheet-fed printers, and is not available in the Windows version.) The test will check standard or oversized projects. If you choose the standard option, this test should result in a printed page with horizontal dots running across where your paper is perforated (this is sometimes called *pinfeed* computer paper). If not, you will need to readjust your paper and try to get the horizontal dots to align with your perforated dots. If you choose the oversized test, the results should be a vertical line at the far left edge of the paper. If not, then you'll have to trim your pages before assembling your finished project. (This testing option is not available on PSD-Windows.)

Number of Copies lets you print up to 99 copies of your project. (Printing the maximum number isn't usually a very good idea, because it could possibly damage your printer by overheating. It also uses up an awful lot of ink ribbons or cartridges.)

Output Size allows you to control the size of your printout, based on percentages. Greeting cards can be sized down, signs and calendars can be sized up or down, and banners and letterheads cannot be sized at all. (PSD-Windows users can choose sizes through the Printer Setup dialog box.)

Paper Feed is an option available if you have a printer that can handle both single sheets of paper and continuous feed. For best results, use continuous feed.

Print Quality allows you to change your printout to different levels of DPI (dots per inch). The formal term for this is *resolution*. Depending upon what kind of printer you have, you can choose how crisp or light your printout is. If you're using NPS, Print Quality lets you print in Draft or Final quality. (If you're using PSD-Windows, you'll find Print Quality in the Printer Setup dialog box.)

Print Backwards is just what it says—an option allowing you to print your project backwards. This isn't available for Windows users, and PSD-Dos users can use this only on sign projects. If you're using your project design to create an iron-on T-shirt, this is an ideal option to use.

Coloring Book Option gives you a printout in outline form, very much like a child's coloring book. This is a good project to try! (Not available on NPS.)

Print Color Samples is useful for those of you who have color printers. PSD-DOS users can print a color chart to see how colors will look.

Check SetUp option will allow you to change your printer setup. (Not available for NPS users.)

Set Contrast Level is a feature for NPS users that sets the printing at one of four levels of contrast. Lower contrast levels reduce wear and tear on your printer ribbons. Lower contrasts are also useful for when you plan to color in your project. Higher contrasts result in darker printouts. (Laser printers will have no use for this option.)

Poster Sized is an option available to PSD-Windows users. It lets you print sign and calendar projects in extra-large sizes.

Help!

Another wonderful feature of the Print Shop programs is the Help function. Just press the F1 key on your keyboard, and the program will provide information or instructions pertaining to the screen you "called for help" from. Figure 1.19 shows an example Help box. Some Help messages are longer than others. To see more of the message, scroll forward or press Enter. When you've finished reading the Help screens, press Esc or select Done.

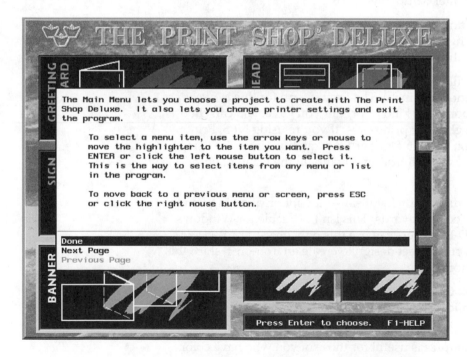

Figure 1.19
A Help box from
PSD-DOS version.

Exiting the Program

Once you've finished a project, select Exit to Main Menu or Return to Main Menu. (Windows users must pull down the File menu and choose Exit.)

When you're back at the Main menu or entry screen, choose Exit. This will take you back to DOS or the Windows Program Manager.

Exit Tip You can exit from within a project by pressing Esc until you reach a menu allowing you an exit to the Main menu.

Onward

Now that you know your way around the Print Shop programs, you're probably ready to try a project. There are hundreds to choose from in this book. Before you get started, read the next section about how to use this book. It will help you interpret any symbols, steps, and illustrations you may encounter.

DEFINITIONS:

blocks Parts of your layout, such as a text block or a graphic block.

click A single quick tap or press of the mouse button.

commands Instructions telling the computer what to do. When you are selecting menu items, you are choosing commands.

cursor The blinking point or line on your screen indicating where you are.

dialog box A box which offers you more information when it appears, or requires more information before a command can be carried out.

double-click Two quick taps or presses of the mouse button.

drag To move an object on-screen to a new location. Point to the object, hold down the left mouse button, and move the mouse until you reach the desired location.

edit To make a change.

continues

continued

elements   Parts of your layout, such as a block of text or a graphic.

file   A storage area for your project.

fonts   The various styles of alphabet letters available as text (also called *typestyles*).

graphics   Any artwork, ruled line, or border.

highlight bar or box   The black box that surrounds your selection. It moves when you move your mouse or press the keyboard arrow keys.

icon   A little on-screen picture.

layout   Details about how your project is set up. A layout designates places for text, art, and borders. It's kind of like having a map of where everything goes.

Main menu   The first screen you see after starting the program.

menu   A box, or pull-down box, that offers selections.

mouse pointer   The arrow on your screen that moves when you move your mouse.

Preview screen   The open area at the right of your screen, showing what the project looks like.

scroll   To move back and forth along a menu or screen.

selection keys   Keys indicated by bold or underlined letters in a menu, that can be pressed with the Alt key to make a selection. Selection keys are shortcuts, often faster than choosing menu items with the arrow keys or mouse.

typestyles   The various styles of alphabet letters available as text (also called *fonts*).

How to Use this Book

It's a good idea to read this short section before starting into the projects in Section 3. You'll see how to use the project pages, and how to read the numbered steps detailing each project. If you need further information about working with text before starting on the project section, see Section 4. If you need more information about working with graphics, see Section 5. If you'd like to see what fonts and art are available on PSD, you'll find them cataloged in the back of the book.

What You'll Find

The projects in Section 3 are divided into twelve parts: Cards, Stationery, Signs and Flyers, Banners, Calendars, Parties and Other Celebrations, Business Projects, School Projects, Home Projects, Other Projects and Crafts, and Kid Stuff.

At the beginning of each of the parts, you'll find "parts pages." These pages will show you the menu sequences necessary for completing each type of project, and provide any special tips for working with the particular project type. The menus pictured on the parts pages are from PSD-DOS. If you're working with PSD-Windows or NPS, you'll find extra information for your particular program too.

On the rest of the pages in Section 3, you'll find various project ideas, one project idea per page. Each project page will contain a title of the idea, a picture of the project, and numbered steps to help you create the project. All of the projects shown were created using the basic PSD program (DOS and Windows versions). If you're using NPS, you'll find steps for creating similar projects using your program.

In addition to these items, you'll also come across boxes with design tips, other ideas for using the project, and important information about the Print Shop programs. Be sure to read these boxes; they'll help you create professional-looking projects, give you suggestions for modifying existing projects, and help spark new ideas.

Section Two

A Project Example

To see an example of how the project steps are set up, take a look at this numbered list from a PSD-DOS idea.

1. Select: • Sign. • Create a New Project. • Tall.

2. Select a **B**ackdrop: • Choose Football Field. • **D**one.

3. Select a Layout: • Choose Football Field 3.

4. Select **F**ill In or Edit.

5. Edit text block: • Tab. • Resize block to make room for a headline at top. • Font: Jester, Font **S**ize: 26-point. • Line **J**ustify: Center, Placement: Center. • Tab. • Type event message, date, and time, five lines, upper and lowercase letters. • Tab. • **D**one.

6. Edit headline block (bottom): • Tab. • Resize block as large as possible across bottom of sign. • Font: Bazooka. • Colors, Text: Black, Shadow: Grey. • Tab. • Type your team's name, all capital letters. • Tab. • **D**one.

7. Select **A**dd New Elements; add: • **H**eadline. Place headline at top of sign, size to fill space. Press Tab and **D**one when finished placing element.

8. Select **F**ill In or Edit.

9. Edit new headline block: • Tab. • Font: Boulder. • **S**hape: Double Arch Up. • Colors, Shadow: Grey. • Tab. • Type **TEAM RALLY!** in all capital letters. • Tab. • **D**one.

Step 1 tells you what menu items to choose as you start each project. Of course, you must begin each project at the Main menu screen. Steps 2 and 3 specify what backdrop and layout to use, if these are required by the project. In this example, you would choose the backdrop art titled "Football Field," and layout number three to go with it. Steps 4–6 tell you how to fill in each layout element. For example, step 6 tells you how to edit a headline block, step by step: choose the font called Bazooka, type in a team name, use capital letters, and create a special effect. Other editing examples will include text size, color, style, and more. Step 7 is an instruction for adding a new element to the layout.

You'll also find selection letters in bold to help you with shortcuts or if you're using the keyboard to help build your projects.

Here's something very important to remember when following instructions for adding new elements: they are only for adding blocks, *not* filling them in. Your PSD program will automatically allow you an opportunity to fill in each new element. You're welcome to do so at that point, but you'll find exact editing details in the numbered steps to come. For our project steps, it's better just to add the elements, and leave them blank until you reach the step for filling them in. In the example shown, step 9 shows you what to do with the new element you've added.

Another important item to note—you won't find numbered steps for saving or printing the project idea. Those steps are always the same, and you'll find them on the parts pages.

If you're using NPS, you'll find numbered lists detailing how you can create projects similar to those shown. Because your program differs from PSD, you won't be able to create the ideas exactly as shown, but you'll find great alternatives.

Ideas

It's a good idea to thumb through all the ideas shown in Section 3. That's a great way of coming up with new ideas of your own. We've tried to compile examples of each kind of project you can make using Print Shop programs, as well as ideas for building other types of projects. Of course, there just isn't enough room to tell you about everything you can build with the Print Shop programs. But we hope the ideas we covered will spark more ideas from you!

The wonderful thing about the Print Shop programs is that you find yourself *being* very creative, even if you don't consider yourself a creative person. These programs make it easy to invent projects.

Every idea in this book can be modified to suit your needs. Experiment, explore, and exhaust all possibilities. No matter what version of the Print Shop programs you have, Apple, DOS, Mac, or Windows, you'll still be able to create your own variations of the projects shown.

Tips, Tips, and More Tips

Throughout Section 3 you'll find boxes with all kinds of tips. You'll also find tips in Sections 4 and 5. And now that we've got your attention here, how about some tips right now?

- When working with fonts, don't try to use too many different kinds in one project. If you require more than one font, choose a second font that contrasts with the first one. Use a *serif* style and a *sans-serif* style (see Section 4). For example, if you're using New Zurica, contrast it with Paramount.

- *Script* fonts—those that look like handwriting or cursive— are sometimes tricky to use. These type styles look best when they are used with upper *and* lowercase letters. It's never a good idea to use a script font with all uppercase letters. It's also not a good idea to use two different kinds of script fonts in the same project.

- Follow the theory that "less is more" for creating professional-looking Print Shop projects. If your layout contains too many blocks of art and text, it will look cluttered and busy.

- Experiment with using different *point sizes* (see Section 4) within your text blocks, within paragraphs and sentences, or even within words. A word with a very large first letter can draw attention to the text. Or try a "ransom-note" technique of using a different style or size for every letter. This technique can be very effective for a headline (but don't overdo it).

- Make sure your text is readable, especially in large projects such as banners.

- Don't be afraid to scale and stretch the art to add interest to your project. This editing technique can create some unique looks.

- Don't neglect color in your projects. If you do not have a color printer, be sure to add color to your project after it's printed out. Markers, paint, colored pencils, and even crayons can help put pizzazz into your printout.

- Just because your project prints out onto a flat piece of

paper doesn't mean your project has to stay flat. You can make all sorts or folded, shaped, and 3-D projects. Use scissors and glue to build onto your project. Cut and paste graphics and text to fashion a project to your liking.

- Try combining several project ideas into one. Or take an existing project and substitute a new graphic or text block to make it into a new idea.

- Combine art, borders, and ruled lines to create new graphic looks. The PSD (DOS and Windows) layering effects will give you lots of flexibility in doing this.

- If you're running out of ideas of your own, skim through magazines and books to find more variations to try.

In Conclusion

You're ready to begin using the project ideas in this book. We've included ideas that range from simple to challenging. Now that you're familiar with how to read the project pages, you're all set. Just remember, when following the numbered steps on each page it's important to note the following:

- Any time you are instructed to add new elements to the project, just create each new block and place it as shown in the picture. You'll find out what to put in each added element in the editing steps that follow.

- You won't find additional steps for saving or printing the project in the numbered list. You can turn to the parts pages at the beginning of each project section to find out how to do these functions.

Good luck—and have fun!

Projects

Section Three

Cards

Card projects can be used for a variety of occasions: invitations, greetings, stationery, customer service responses, announcements, holidays, and much more. Here are the basic steps for creating any card using PSD. If you're using the Windows version, steps 8–13 will vary slightly.

1. Select Greeting Card project from the Main menu screen.

2. Select Create a New project. (Not in PSD-Windows.)

3. Select the project orientation.

4. Select a Backdrop.

5. Choose a backdrop graphic design.

6. Select a Layout.

7. Choose a layout design.

8. Select Fill in or Edit.

9. Fill in each layout element.

10. Select Go to Inside of Card. Repeat steps 4–9.

11. Optional: Select Go to Back of Card. Repeat steps 6–9.

12. Save the project. Select Save from the menu list and type in a file name.

13. Print the project. Select Print from the menu list. Choose your printer options and select Print.

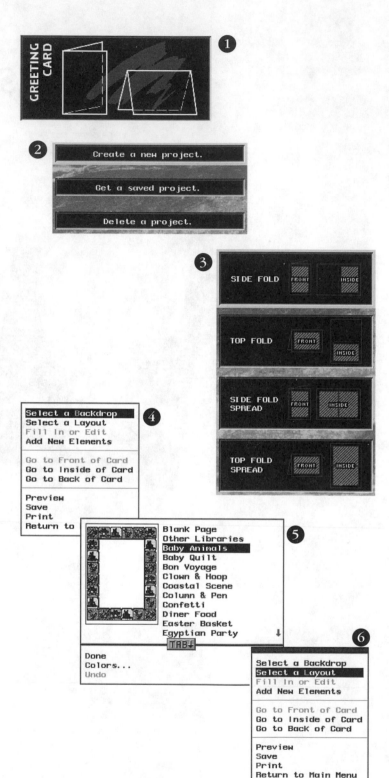

If you've not read the "How To Use This Book" section (Section 2) yet, it would be a good idea to do so now. You'll find out how to follow the different project steps. If you have any problems editing text or graphic blocks, refer to Section 4 and Section 5.

PSD-Windows Step 8 will look different on your screen. You'll use the Tool Palette, and pull down menus from the Menu bar to help you fill in each layout element. To follow steps 10 and 11, pull down the **P**roject menu from the Menu bar to select **I**nside of Card or **B**ack of Card. You can also click on the Navigation button in the bottom right corner of your screen. (This button has two directional arrows to take you to each side of the card.) To follow steps 12 and 13, pull down the **F**ile menu to make selections.

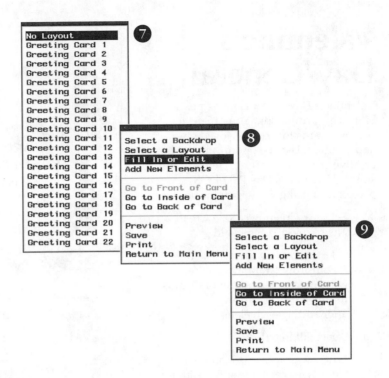

You will find different steps to follow after step 3:

4. Select Border and choose a border graphic if desired.

5. Select Graphic and choose a layout and art.

6. Select Message, choose a font and style, and type in your text.

7. Select Inside of Card, and repeat steps 4–6.

8. Select Save from the menu, and save your project.

9. Select Print from the menu to print your project.

You'll be able to add text to the back of the card by selecting the Give Yourself Credit option from the Print/Save menu. (This is only available if you print the card at 100% size.)

You'll also find (in step 2) an option to select a Ready-Made card. Your NPS program has a collection of cards that are ready to print and use, or add your own personal touch to them. For the card projects in this section, you will create your own.

Valentine's Day/General

Valentine's Day presents many possibilities in cardmaking. You can design personal cards for friends, loved ones, and children. Use the opportunity to be creative, serious, or funny. Here's a simple Valentine's Day PSD-DOS project idea using a row graphic border.

1. Select: • Greeting card. • Create a New Project. • Side Fold.

2. Select **A**dd New Elements; add: • Four **R**ow Graphics. You're going to create a border of Cupids in step 4. Select Tab and **D**one after adding each element.

3. Select **F**ill In or Edit.

4. Edit row graphics: • Choose Cupids for each one and position the blocks as shown in illustration. • **M**ove one graphic to top of card. • Place another graphic at bottom. • **R**otate third graphic and place on left side of card. • **R**otate remaining graphic and place on right side of card. • **M**ove each row closer together to form border of Cupids. • Choose **D**one after completing each graphic.

5. Select **A**dd New Elements; add: • **T**ext Block. Place block in middle of Cupid border. • **D**one.

6. Select **F**ill In or Edit.

7. Edit text block: • Tab • Resize block to fill middle of Cupid border. • **F**ont: Scribble, Font **S**ize: Medium. • Line **J**ustify: Center, Placement: Center. • Tab. • Type "HAPPY VALENTINE'S DAY!", three lines, all uppercase letters. • Tab. • **D**one.

8. Select Inside of Card.

9. Select a **B**ackdrop: • Choose Lips! Lips!. • **D**one.

10. Select a-Layout: • Choose Greeting Card 4.

11. Select **F**ill In or Edit.

12. Edit border: • Choose Eight Point. • **D**one.

13. Edit text block: • Tab. • **F**ont: Boulder, Font **S**ize: Large. • Line **J**ustify: Center, Placement: Center. • Tab. • Type "To A Real Sweetie!", two lines, upper- and lowercase letters. • Tab. • **D**one.

Design Tip

Valentine cards are great for gluing on extra effects. Using a clear-drying glue, try adding glitter, bows, dried flowers, lace, and other decorative touches to make a keepsake card that will always be remembered.

Mother's Day/ General

Mother's Day is one of the most popular days of the year to give a card. Here's your chance to personalize a Mother's Day card to really say what you're thinking. The PSD-Windows project below is a good example of keeping a theme in your card design. The front uses the Butterflies backdrop, and the inside uses the Wildflowers square graphic. Both complement each other very well.

1. Select: • **Greeting Card.** • **Top Fold.**

2. Select a Backdrop: • Choose Butterflies. • Click OK.

3. Select a Layout: • Choose Greeting Card 7. • Click OK.

4. Edit border: • Double-click on border frame. • Choose Eight Point. • Click OK.

5. Edit bottom headline block: • Double-click block. • **F**ont: Paramount, **S**hape: Rectangle. • Type "Happy Mother's Day!", upper- and lowercase letters. • Click OK. (Don't edit top headline block or square graphic block, just leave them blank or delete them.)

6. Select **I**nside of Card.

7. Select a Backdrop: • Choose Blank Page. • Click OK.

8. Select a Layout: • Choose No Layout. • Click OK.

9. Use the New Object tool to add: • **B**order. • **S**quare Graphic. • **T**ext Block. Resize the square graphic as large as possible and place in lower left corner. Place the text block in the upper right corner, size as shown in illustration.

10. Edit border: • Double-click border frame. • Choose Eight Point. • Click OK.

11. Edit graphic: • Double-click graphic. • Choose Wildflowers. • Click OK.

12. Edit text block: • Double-click block. • **F**ont: Paramount, Size: Small, Justification: **H**orizontal Center. • Type "Moms like you are rather rare, Giving all your love and care, So on this day we want to share, Our appreciation to one so fair.", six lines, upper- and lowercase letters. • Click OK.

Design Tip

Unless you have a color printer, don't forget to add color to your card projects. Try colored pencils, markers, or water colors.

Cards

Father's Day/ General

Don't forget to give Dad a personalized card on Father's Day. This PSD-Windows project emphasizes the fishing graphic motif.

1. Select: • **G**reeting Card. • **S**ide **F**old Spread.

2. Select a Backdrop: • Choose Blank Page. • Click OK.

3. Select a Layout: • Choose No Layout. • Click OK.

4. Use the New Object tool to add: • **B**order. • **S**quare Graphic. • **H**eadline. Position headline at top, within border, and resize to fill top space as shown in illustration. Place square graphic beneath headline and enlarge to fill remaining space, as large as possible.

5. Edit border: • Double-click border frame. • Choose Four Point. • Click OK.

6. Edit headline block: • Double-click block. • Font: Jester, Style: Bold on. • Shape: Arc Up. • Customize: Effect 11, scroll the scroll box until you reach effect 11 on the Customize bar. (PSD-DOS users can use edit commands to create an effect similar to the effect shown.) • Type "Sit back and relax, Dad", upper- and lowercase letters. • Click OK.

7. Edit square graphic: • Double-click block. • Choose Adirondack Chair. • Click OK.

8. Select **I**nside of Card.

9. Select a Backdrop: • Choose Fishing. • Click OK.

10. Select a Layout: • Choose No Layout. • Click OK.

11. Use the New Object tool from the tool palette to add: • **H**eadline Block. • **T**ext Block. Place headline at top of project and stretch across space as shown in illustration. Place text block in lower left corner and size to fit as shown.

12. Edit headline block: • Double-click block. • Font: Jester, Style: Bold on. • Type "It's Father's Day!", upper- and lowercase letters. • Click OK.

13. Edit text block: • Double-click block. • Font: Jester, Style: Bold on, Size: Small, Justification: Horizontal Center. • Type "So take it easy, enjoy the day, Do a little fishing down on the bay, Catch a little guppy if you may, Then tell us how huge it really did weigh!", upper- and lowercase letters, four lines. • Click OK.

Sympathy/ General

For a simple, yet elegant sympathy card, follow the steps in this PSD-DOS project idea.

1. Select: • Greeting Card. • Create a New Project. • Side Fold.

2. Select **A**dd New Elements; add: • **B**order. • **M**ini-border. • **T**ext Block. Place the mini-border inside the large border and size as shown in example. Place the text block inside the mini-border. Select Tab and **D**one after placing each element.

3. Select **F**ill In or Edit.

4. Edit border: • Choose Lines & Diamonds, Large. • **D**one.

5. Edit text block: • Tab. • **F**ont: Signature, Font **S**ize: Medium. • Line **J**ustify: Center, **P**lacement: Center. • Tab. • Type "Sincerest Sympathies", upper- and lowercase letters, two lines. • Tab. • **D**one.

6. Edit mini-border: • Choose Lines & Diamonds, Large. • **S**cale border to fit around text block in center of card. • **D**one.

7. Select **I**nside of Card.

8. Select **A**dd New Elements; add: • **B**order. • **T**ext Block. Size text block to fill entire space within border. Select Tab and **D**one after choosing each element.

9. Select **F**ill In or Edit.

10. Edit border: • Choose Lines & Diamonds, Large. • **D**one.

11. Edit text block: • Tab. • **F**ont: Signature, Font **S**ize: Medium. • Line **J**ustify: Center, **P**lacement: Center. • Tab. • Type "Our condolences to you and your family", upper- and lowercase letters, three lines. • Tab. • **D**one.

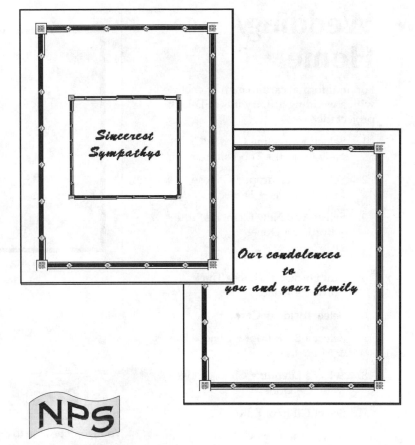

You won't be able to duplicate the project shown, but follow these steps to create an elegant sympathy card.

1. Select: • Greeting Card. • Design Your Own. • Side Fold.

2. Select Border: • Choose wide, Lilies.

3. Select Message: • Choose Merced, Solid. • Type "In Sympathy", two lines, upper- and lowercase letters. • Press F8 to center.

4. Select Inside of Card.

5. Select Message: • Choose Merced, Solid. • Type "Please know that we are thinking of you in your time of sorrow.", upper- and lowercase letters. • Press F8 to center.

Wedding/ Home

For an informal card to mail or enclose with a wedding gift, try this PSD-DOS project idea.

1. Select: • Greeting Card. • Create a New Project. • Top Fold Spread.

2. Select a **B**ackdrop: • Choose French Horns. • **D**one.

3. Select **A**dd New Elements; add: • **B**order. • **D**one.

4. Select **F**ill In or Edit.

5. Edit border: • Choose Thick Border. • **D**one.

6. Select Inside of Card.

7. Select a **B**ackdrop: • Choose Doves & Mint. • **D**one.

8. Select a **L**ayout: • Choose Doves & Mint 3. • **D**one.

9. Select **F**ill In or Edit.

10. Edit headline block 1 (top): • Tab. • **F**ont: Sherwood. • **J**ustify: Center. • Tab. • Type "Congratulations!", upper- and lowercase letters. • **D**one.

11. Edit text block: • Tab. • **F**ont: Calligrapher, Font **S**ize: Small. • Line **J**ustify: Center, **P**lacement: Center. • Tab. • Type "May you have a blessed marriage, One that's sure to grow, Full of warmth and happiness, And love that makes you glow.", eight lines, upper- and lowercase letters. • **D**one.

12. Edit headline block 2 (bottom): • Tab. • **F**ont: Sherwood. • Line **J**ustify: Center. • Tab. • Type "Best Wishes!", upper- and lowercase letters. • Tab. • **D**one.

You won't be able to create the same wedding card shown, but here are some steps for an attractive alternative.

1. Select: • Greeting Card. • Design Your Own. • Side Fold.

2. Select Graphics: • Choose Small Corners, Graphics, Daisies.

3. Select Message: • Choose Lassen font, Solid. • Type "A Wedding Wish", 3 lines, upper- and lowercase. • Press F8 to center message in space. • Press F10 to preview front of card.

4. Select Inside of Card.

5. Select Border: • Choose Thin, Frilly.

6. Select Message: • Choose Small, Solid. • Type same message as PSD project. • Press FP to center.

Design Tip

If you're using poems or prose in your card, be sure to separate lines where necessary. If you need to indent, insert 3–5 blank spaces before a line starts.

Anniversary/ Business

Here's a PSD-Windows project idea for a business anniversary card.

1. Select: • **Greeting Card.** • Side **F**old Spread.

2. Select a Backdrop: • Choose Confetti. • Click OK.

3. Select a Layout: • Choose Confetti 4. • Click OK.

4. Edit mini-border: • Double-click mini-border. • Choose Celtic, Small. • Click OK.

5. Edit text block 1 (inside mini-border): • Double-click block. • **Font:** Calligrapher, Size: Medium, Justification: **H**orizontal Center. • Type name of company and "is proud to announce our 75th anniversary!" (substitute your company's anniversary year) in upper- and lowercase letters. • Click OK.

6. Edit text block 2: • Double-click block. • **Font:** Signature, Size: 20-point, Justification: **H**orizontal Center. • Type "Join us in Celebrating!", two lines, upper- and lowercase. • Click OK.

7. Select Inside of Card.

8. Select a Backdrop: • Choose Hourglass. • Click OK.

9. Select a Layout: • Choose Hourglass 5. • Click OK.

10. Edit border: • Click border. • Use the Delete tool from the tool palette to delete border.

11. Edit headline block 1: • Double-click block. • **Font:** Standout. • Type "ANNIVERSARY SALE!", uppercase letters. • Click OK.

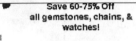

12. Edit headline block 2 (in the hourglass): • Double-click block. • **Font:** New Zurica. • Type "75 Years", upper- and lowercase letters. • Click OK.

13. Edit text block 1: • Resize block to take up small space at top of card, as shown in example. • Double-click block. • **Font:** New Zurica, Style: Bold on, Size: Small. • Type "Special Anniversary Savings for all our valued Customers!", two lines, upper- and lowercase letters. • Click OK.

14. Edit text block 2: • Resize block to take up more space, as shown in example. • Double-click block. • **Font:** New Zurica, Style: Bold on, Size: Small. • Type savings message, date, and time of anniversary open house. • Click OK.

Cards

New Baby/ Home

Welcome new arrivals to the family with a personally-designed card. Follow these PSD-DOS steps:

1. Select: • Greeting Card. • Create a New Project. • Top Fold.

2. Select a **B**ackdrop: • Choose Baby Things. • **D**one.

3. Select a **L**ayout: • Choose Baby Things 5.

4. Select **F**ill In or Edit: • Delete all text blocks except the circle headline appearing in the baby rattle at left. To delete, edit each block, Tab and select **D**elete. Select **D**one after deleting each element.

5. Edit headline (in rattle): • Tab. • Font: Jester. • Tab. • Type "New Baby", upper- and lowercase letters. • Tab. • **D**one.

6. Select **A**dd New Elements; add: • Two **H**eadlines. • Place each headline so that they are positioned opposite each other vertically on right side of baby rattle art. Tab and select **D**one after adding each element.

7. Select **F**ill In or Edit.

8. Edit headline 1 (top): • Tab. • Font: Jester. • Shape: Arc up. • **J**ustify: Center. • Tab. • Type "Congratulations!", upper- and lowercase letters. • Tab. • **D**one.

9. Edit headline 2 (bottom): • Tab. • Font: Jester. • Shape: Bottom Arch. • Tab. • Type "It's a Boy!" or "It's a Girl!", upper- and lowercase letters. • Tab. • **D**one.

10. Select Inside of Card.

11. Select a **L**ayout: • Choose Greeting Card 9.

12. Select **F**ill In or Edit.

13. Edit border: • Choose Balls & Blocks. • **D**one.

14. Edit square graphic block 1 (top): • Choose Teddy. • **D**one.

15. Edit square graphic block 2 (bottom): • Choose Teddy. • **D**one.

16. Edit headline block: • Tab. • Font: Heather. • Tab. • Type "Can't wait to see him!" or "Can't wait to see her!", upper- and lowercase letters. • Tab. • **D**one.

Open House/ School

Open House invitations can be used for new home owners, real estate showings, new businesses, clubs, and more. This PSD-Windows project idea is for a school open house.

1. Select: • Greeting Card. • Side Fold Spread.

2. Select a Backdrop: • Choose Blank Page. • Click OK.

3. Select a Layout: • Choose No Layout. • Click OK.

4. Use the New Object tool from the tool palette to add: • Four Row Graphics.

5. Edit row graphics: • Double-click a block. • Choose ABC 123 art and select Apply to All (to apply to all four graphic blocks). • Click OK. • Move one graphic row to top of card. • Move another row to bottom. • Rotate third graphic 90 degrees, and place at left of card. • Rotate remaining graphic 270 degrees, and place at right of card. • Move all four rows together to form a square border, as shown in example.

6. Use the New Object tool to add: • Text Block. • Place block in center of card, inside square border created in step 5.

7. Edit text block: • Double-click block. • Font: Heather, Size: Medium, Justification: Horizontal Center. • Type "PTO Open House", three lines. • Click OK.

8. Select Inside of Card.

9. Select a Backdrop: • Choose Blank Page. • Click OK.

10. Select a Layout: • Choose No Layout. • Click OK.

11. Use the New Object tool to add: • Two Text Blocks. • Row Graphic. • Place row graphic across top of card and size as large as possible. Place one text block on left side of card, filling remaining space. Place the other text block on right side of card, filling remaining space.

12. Edit row graphic block: • Double-click block. • Choose ABC 123. • Click OK.

13. Edit text block 1 (left): • Double-click block. • Font: Librarian. • Size: Make first four lines Medium size. Make date and time lines Small size. • Type "Parent/ Teacher Organization presents Fall Open House", and add date and time. • Click OK.

14. Edit text block 2 (right): • Double-click block. • Repeat the same directions followed for step 13, but type your own message. • Click OK when finished.

Cards

Announcement/ Home

Announcement cards can be used for a range of projects, whether you're advertising special sales promotions to valued clients or updating family and friends on a recent marriage. Here's a PSD-DOS idea for a semi-formal wedding announcement with a reception.

1. Select: • Greeting Card. • Create a New Project. • Top Fold.

2. Select a Layout: • Choose Greeting Card 25.

3. Select Fill In or Edit.

4. Edit border: • Choose Spring Border. • Done.

5. Edit text block: • Tab. • Font: Calligrapher, Font Size: Small. • Line Justify: Center, Placement: Center. • Tab. • Type "Mr. and Mrs. (*name of the parents*) proudly announce the marriage of their daughter (*name of the daughter*) to (*name of the groom*)", upper- and lowercase letters. • Tab. • Done.

6. Select Inside of Card.

7. Select a Layout: • Choose Greeting Card 25.

8. Select Fill In or Edit.

9. Edit border: • Choose Spring Border. • Done.

10. Edit text block: • Tab. • Font: Calligrapher, Font Size: Small. • Line Justify: Center, Placement: Center. • Tab. • Type "Please join them in a reception celebrating this occasion Saturday, October 16, nineteen hundred and ninety three at half past 3 o'clock at their home, 108 Delancey Street, Millville,

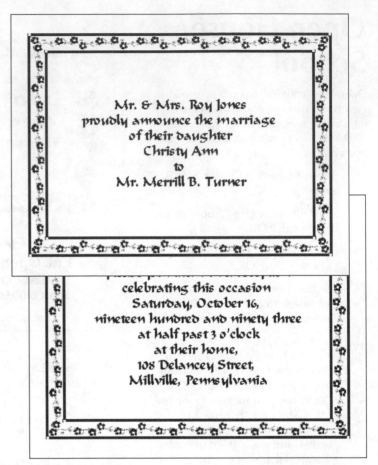

Pennsylvania" (using your own dates, time, and place), upper- and lowercase letters. Follow line breaks similar to those shown in example. • Tab. • Done.

Other PSD Card Ideas   Follow these tips to create a birth announcement.

1. Choose side fold orientation.

2. Choose Baby Animals backdrop and layout 5.

3. Use Scribble, Medium size to type "There's a new kid on the block!", upper- and lowercase letters.

4. For the inside of card, choose same backdrop and layout; add information about baby's name, parents, birth date, and birth weight.

Design Tip

Typestyles that resemble handwriting, or script, work best for formal and semi-formal occasions. Using both upper- and lowercase letters will give you a more professional-looking card. When dealing with formal events, it's best to keep the design crisp and simple, such as using an elegant border and typestyle.

Graduation/ Home

Parents, grandparents, family, friends, school faculty, and businesses will all find designing a graduation card a simple project to complete. The following example was created on PSD-Windows.

1. Select: • **Greeting Card**. • **Side Fold** Spread.

2. Select a Backdrop: • Choose **Blank** Page. • Click OK.

3. Select a Layout: • Choose **Greeting Card 25**. • Click OK.

4. Edit bottom headline: • Click block. • Use the Delete tool from the tool palette to delete headline block.

5. Edit border: • Double-click block. • Choose Diamond Corners. • Click OK.

6. Edit square graphic block: • Enlarge the block to fill space, as shown in illustration. • Double-click block. • Choose Graduation. • Click OK.

7. Edit headline: • Resize block to fill space, as shown in illustration. • Double-click block. • **Font:** Paramount, Bold on. • **Shape:** Double Arch Up. • Type "Congratulations!", upper- and lowercase letters. • Click OK.

8. Select **Inside of Card**.

9. Select a Backdrop: • Choose Graduation Caps. • Click OK.

10. Select a Layout: • Choose Graduation Caps 4. • Click OK.

11. Edit text block: • Double-click block. • **Font:** Paramount, Style: Bold on, Size: Small. • Type "Best Wishes to you in all your future endeavors!", upper- and lowercase letters. • Click OK.

12. Edit headline: • Double-click block. • **Font:** Paramount. • **Shape:** Perspective Left. • **Justify:** Center. • **Customize:** Effect 1. Move the customize scroll bar to the left to find effect 1 (normal-looking type). • Type "You Finally Made It!", upper- and lowercase letters. • Click OK.

Other PSD Card Ideas Follow these tips to create a school-oriented graduation card.

1. Choose top fold spread orientation.

2. Design a front with a simple border, such as Medallion, and a text block.

3. Inside, use the Watch and Confetti backdrop and layout 5 to create a message of congratulations from the school faculty and staff.

Cards

Just Moved/ Home

Whether you've moved your family or your business, you can design a card to alert everyone to your change of address. Here's a PSD-DOS project idea for a "Just Moved" card.

1. Select: • Greeting Card. • Create a New Project. • Top Fold.

2. Select a **B**ackdrop: • Choose Stained Glass. • **D**one.

3. Select a **L**ayout: • Choose Stained Glass 1.

4. Select **F**ill In or Edit.

5. Edit text block: • Tab. • **F**ont: Calligrapher, Font Size: 52-point. • Line Justify: Center, Placement: Center. • Tab. • Type "We've Moved!", two lines, upper- and lowercase letters. • Tab. • **D**one.

6. Select **I**nside of Card.

7. Select a **L**ayout: • Choose Greeting Card 25.

8. Select **F**ill In or Edit.

9. Edit border: • Choose Lines & Diamonds. • **D**one.

10. Edit text block: • Tab. • **F**ont: Calligrapher, Font **S**ize: Medium. • Line **J**ustify: Center, Placement: Center. • Tab. • Type "Here's our new address:", leave a blank line, type your name and new address. • Tab. • **D**one.

Other PSD Card Ideas Is your business relocating? Create a "We Moved" announcement to send to your customers.

1. Choose top fold spread orientation.

2. Design a front with a simple border, headline, text block with company name, and a small graphic.

3. Inside, use Fireworks backdrop and layout 4 to create a new location address and sales information.

Party Invitation/ Child

The Print Shop programs are perfect for creating your own party invitations: birthday parties, cookouts, New Year's Eve parties, holiday gatherings, dinner parties, office parties, school parties, and much more. The PSD-Windows project shown on this page is a classic children's birthday party invitation, with traditional clown art.

1. Select: • **Greeting Card.** • **Top Fold Spread.**

2. Select a Backdrop: • Choose **Clown with Card.** • Click OK.

3. Select a Layout: • Choose **Clown with Card 1.** • Click OK.

4. Edit text block: • Double-click block. • **Font:** Standout, **Style:** Shadow on, **Size:** Large. • Type "IT'S A PARTY!", uppercase letters, three lines. • Click OK.

5. Select **Inside of Card.**

6. Select a Backdrop: • Choose **Clown & Confetti.** • Click OK.

7. Select a Layout: • Choose **Clown & Confetti 4.** • Click OK.

8. Edit headline: • Double-click block. • **Font:** New Zurica. • Type "You're Invited!", upper- and lowercase letters. • Click OK.

9. Edit text block 1 (left): • Double-click block. • **Font:** Jester, **Style:** Bold on, **Size:** 20-point. • Type "Bobby Miller is turning 6!" (substitute your child's name), upper- and lowercase letters. • Click OK.

10. Edit text block 2: • Double-click block. • **Font:** Subway, **Size:** Medium. • Type "Come to Bobby's Birthday Party, Friday, November 12 from 3–5!" (substitute your child's name, date, and time of party), upper- and lowercase letters. • Click OK.

Cards

Thank You/ Business

Need to thank someone for a job well done? Need to extend special thanks to a friend or customer? Thank-you cards are useful around the home, school, or office. Here's a PSD-DOS business thank-you card project that can be sent to customers.

1. Select: • Greeting Card. • Create a New Project. • Side Fold Spread.

2. Select a **B**ackdrop: • Choose Gradient Cone. • **D**one.

3. Select **A**dd New Elements; add: • **H**eadline Block. • **T**ext Block. Place headline block at top of card as shown in illustration. Place text block at bottom of card. • Select Tab and **D**one after inserting each element.

4. Select **F**ill In or Edit.

5. Edit headline: • Tab. • **F**ont: Moderne. • Tab. • Type "THANKS!", uppercase letters. • Tab. • **D**one.

6. Edit text block: • Tab. • **F**ont: Moderne, Font **S**ize: Small. • Line **J**ustify: Center, **P**lacement: Center. • Tab. • Type "on behalf of Johnson Electricians, Inc." (substitute your company name), upper- and lowercase letters. • Tab. • **D**one.

7. Select Inside of Card.

8. Select a **B**ackdrop: • Choose Gradient. • **D**one.

9. Select a **L**ayout: • Choose Gradient 5.

10. Select **F**ill In or Edit.

11. Edit headline: • Tab. • **F**ont: Moderne. • Tab. • Type "Your business means a lot to us!",

upper- and lowercase letters, two lines. • **D**one.

12. Edit text block 1 (left): • Tab. • Font: Moderne, Font **S**ize: Small. • Line **J**ustify: Center, **P**lacement: Center. • Tab. • Type "Thanks for putting your trust in our company. Quality is our Number One concern, and we want to make our customers the happiest customers around. We hope our service was more than satisfactory.", upper- and lowercase letters. • Tab. • **D**one.

13. Edit text block 2 (right): • Tab. • Font: Moderne, Font **S**ize: Small for the paragraph, Medium for the phone number. • Line **J**ustify: Left, **P**lacement: Center. • Tab. • Type "If there are any suggestions or questions concerning Johnson Electricians, Inc., please give us a call and we'll respond right away! Thanks again. 777-0000", (substitute your company name), upper- and lowercase letters. • Tab. • **D**one.

Family Reunion/Home

Family reunions can be formal or fun. Try this PSD-Windows project idea for a fun reunion picnic during the Fourth of July holiday.

1. Select: • **Greeting Card.** • **Top Fold.**

2. Select a Backdrop: • Choose Kids. • Click OK.

3. Select a Layout: • Choose Kids 4. • Click OK.

4. Edit headline: • Double-click block. • Font: Bazooka. • Type "SMITH FAMILY REUNION" (substitute your family name), uppercase letters. • Click OK.

5. Edit text block: • Double-click block. • Font: Jester, Size: Medium, Justification: Horizontal Center. • Type "The Event You've All Been Waiting For!", two lines, upper- and lowercase letters. • Click OK.

6. Select Inside of Card.

7. Select a Backdrop: • Choose Blank Page. • Click OK.

8. Select a Layout: • Choose Greeting Card 7. • Click OK.

9. Edit square graphic: • Click on graphic. • Use the Delete tool to delete graphic.

10. Edit bottom headline: • Click on block. • Use the Delete tool to delete bottom headline.

11. Edit border: • Double-click border frame. • Choose Stars & Stripes. • Click OK.

12. Edit headline: • Font: Jester. • Type "Join Us for Our Annual Reunion Picnic!", upper- and lowercase letters. • Click OK. You may have to resize block to fill space, as shown in example.

13. Use the New Object tool to add: • **Text Block.** Place block beneath headline block, size to fill remaining space.

14. Edit text block: • Double-click block. • Using different fonts, as shown in illustration, type in your reunion details. • Click OK.

Cards

Friendship/ Home

While you can certainly go to any card store and find dozens of all-occasion cards, there's something to be said for designing one from the heart. Here's a PSD-DOS project idea for a light-hearted friendship card.

1. Select: • Greeting Card. • Create a New Project. • Side Fold.

2. Select a Backdrop: • Choose Sheep in Field. • Done.

3. Select a Layout: • Choose Sheep in Field 5.

4. Select Fill In or Edit.

5. Delete all blocks except the last block, tilted in bottom right corner. To delete, edit each block, Tab, select Delete, and Done.

6. Edit text block (bottom right corner): • Tab. • Font: Jester, Font Size: 14-point. • Line Justify: Center, Placement: Center. • Tab. • Type "I Can Always Count on Ewe!", upper- and lowercase letters, two lines. • Tab. • Done.

7. Select Inside of Card.

8. Select a Layout: • Choose Greeting Card 4.

9. Select Fill In or Edit.

10. Edit border: • Choose Blue Check. • Done.

11. Edit text block: • Tab. • Font: Jester, Font Size: Medium. • Line Justify: Center, Placement: Top. • Type "Thanks for being such a good friend!", upper- and lowercase letters, three lines. • Tab. • Done.

Follow these steps for an adult friendship card.

1. Select: • Greeting Card. • Design Your Own. • Side Fold.

2. Select Graphic: • Choose Small Frame, Coffee.

3. Select Message: • Choose Amador, Solid. • Type "A Cup of Coffee", three lines.

4. Select Inside of Card.

5. Select Border: • Choose Thin, Ribbon.

6. Select Message: • Choose Amador, Solid. • Type "And a Good Friend like you—two of my favorite things!" • Press F8 to center.

Customer Service Response/Business

Many businesses today use customer response cards to evaluate their service. Here's a PSD-Windows project that offers a professional-looking card you can distribute to all your clients.

1. Select: • **Greeting Card.** • **Top Fold Spread.**

2. Select a Backdrop: • Choose Blank Page. • Click OK.

3. Select a Layout: • Choose No Layout. • Click OK.

4. Use the New Object tool to add: • **Border.** • **Square Graphic.** • Two **Text Blocks.** Place one text block at the top of the project, size to fill space as shown in illustration. Place square graphic below text block 1, size to fill middle space as shown in illustration. Place last text block below square graphic, size to fill remaining space.

5. Edit border: • Double-click border frame. • Choose Diamond Corners. • Click OK.

6. Edit square graphic: • Double-click block. • Choose Lily Ornament. • Click OK.

7. Edit text block 1 (top): • Double-click block. • Font: NewZurica, Style: Bold on, Size: Medium, Justify: Horizontal Center. • Type name of company, upper- and lowercase letters. • Click OK.

8. Edit text block 2 (bottom): • Double-click block. • Font: Boulder, Size: Medium Justify: Horizontal Center. • Type "CUSTOMER RESPONSE CARD", all uppercase letters. • Click OK.

9. Select Inside of Card.

10. Use the New Object tool to add: • Four **Text Blocks.** Place the first block at top of project, size small. Place block 2 below first block, size to fit name and address, as shown in example. Place block 3 below block 2, size to include questionnaire. Place final block at bottom, small size.

11. Using different fonts and point sizes, type in text pertaining to your company's customer service response card in each text block. Use the example shown to help you. • Click OK when finished.

Cards

Baby Shower/ Home

Shower invitations for babies or brides are made simply, using PSD-DOS steps like these.

1. Select: • Greeting Card. • Create a New Project. • Side Fold.

2. Select a **B**ackdrop: • Choose Baby Quilt. • **D**one.

3. Select a Layout: • Choose Baby Quilt 10.

4. Select **F**ill In or Edit.

5. Edit border: • Tab. • Delete border. • **D**one.

6. Edit headline block: • Tab. • Font: NewZurica. • Tab. • Type "It's Time For . . .", upper- and lowercase letters. • Tab. • **D**one.

7. Edit text block: • Tab. • Font: Boulder, Font Size: Large, Style: Drop Shadow. • Tab. • Type "A Baby Shower!", three lines, upper- and lowercase letters. • **D**one.

8. Select Inside of Card.

9. Select a **B**ackdrop: • Choose Baby Quilt. • **D**one.

10. Select **A**dd New Elements; add: • **T**ext Block. Remember to Tab, and select **D**one after adding element.

11. Select **F**ill In or Edit.

12. Edit text block: • Tab. • Font: NewZurica, Font **S**ize: Medium. • Tab. • Type "Join us for a Baby Shower for" and add name of person, date, time, address, and phone number.• **D**one.

13. Optional: • Select **B**ack of Card.

14. Select a Layout: • Choose Greeting Card 1. • **D**one.

15. Select **F**ill In or Edit.

16. Edit graphic block: • Choose Ink Swash. • **D**one.

17. Edit text block: • Tab. • **M**ove text block closer to graphic. • Font: Scribble, Font **S**ize: X-small. • Tab. • Type "Spiffy Cards." • Tab. • **D**one.

Design Tip

Whenever you're working with script type, like Signature, always use upper- and lowercase letters for a professional look. Never use all caps.

Notecard/ Personal

The notecards you design on the Print Shop programs can be used the same way as those you purchase in a card shop. Place graphics and borders on the fronts of the cards, and leave the insides blank for personal messages. Follow these PSD-Windows steps to see how.

1. Select: • **G**reeting Card. • **S**ide Fold.

2. Select a Backdrop: • Choose Fruit and Leaves. • Click OK.

3. Select a Layout: • Choose No Layout. • Click OK.

4. Optional: • Select **B**ack of Card.

5. Select a Layout: • Choose Greeting Card 1. • Click OK.

6. Edit graphic block: • Double-click block. • Choose Chickens. • Click OK.

7. Edit text block: • **F**ont: Calligraphy font, Size: Small, Justification: Horizontal Center. • Type your name or phrase, such as "Nancy's Notecards." • Click OK.

Gift Idea   Print out 8–10 copies of your personally-designed notecards. Match them up with envelopes, package them in a pretty box, and you've got a perfect gift to give!

Create notecards by selecting graphics or borders for the front of the card and leave the inside blank, as these steps show:

1. Select: • Greeting Card. • Design Your Own. • Side Fold.

2. Select Graphic: • Choose Small Frame, Graphics, Daisies.

3. Print your project, and you've got a perfect notecard.

Design Tip

Notecards are perfect for personalizing with monograms, initials, and names. For example, use the script fonts to produce elegant initials to place in the center of the notecard border in the example just outlined.

Stationery

Stationery designed with the Print Shop programs can be used for businesses, schools, clubs, and home. You'll find uses such as special sales announcement letters for your customers, holiday letterhead, a one-page family newsletter, or school progress reports. Here are the basic steps for creating any letterhead using PSD. If you're using the Windows version, steps 8–11 will vary slightly.

1. Select Letterhead project from the Main menu screen.

2. Select Create a New Project. (Not on PSD-Windows.)

3. Select the project orientation.

4. Select a Backdrop.

5. Choose a graphic design, if desired.

6. Select a Layout.

7. Choose the layout design.

8. Select Fill in or Edit.

9. Fill in each layout element.

10. Save the project. Select Save from the menu list, and type in the file name.

11. Print the project. Select Print from the menu list. Choose the printer options and select Print.

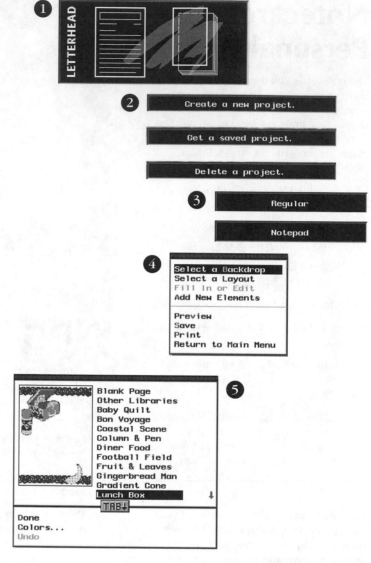

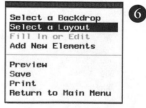

Letterhead projects come in two size orientations: regular (called Single Page on PSD-Windows) and notepad. Regular is a standard 8 1/2-by-11-inch letter size. Notepad is a 5 1/2-by-8 1/2-inch size. Notepad projects are printed two to a page.

Most letterheads you are accustomed to seeing have a *masthead* at the top, which is a block containing a company name, address, and sometimes a logo. There are many variations in letterhead designs, as a glance through the numerous PSD layouts will reveal. Many companies print up letterheads and envelopes to match. You can take your designs to a professional printer and do the same!

Notepads are a wonderful way to express written communication. Once you've designed a notepad that fits your needs, take it to a printer and have it made into a real notepad of paper. It's easy to do.

PSD-Windows Step 8 will differently on your screen. You'll find the Tool Palette and pull-down menus from the Menu bar to help you fill in each layout element. To follow steps 10 and 11, pull down the **F**ile menu to make selections to **S**ave and **P**rint.

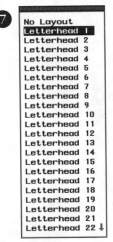

You will find different steps to follow after step 2:

3. Select Graphic and choose a layout and art.

4. Select Text; choose a font and style, and type in the text.

5. Select Ruled Line and choose a horizontal line, if desired.

6. Select Bottom of Letterhead.

7. Repeat steps 3–5 to design the bottom of the letterhead project.

8. Select Save from the menu and save your project.

9. Select Print from the menu to print your project.

Letterhead/ Business

Letterhead is essential for any professional correspondence, whether it be for business, school, community organizations, or clubs. Letterhead is also useful for personal correspondence, for adults and children alike. The following PSD-DOS example shows how to create a professional business letterhead.

1. Select: • Letterhead. • Create a New Project. • Regular.

2. Select a Layout: • Choose Letterhead 37.

3. Select Fill In or Edit.

4. Edit square graphic: • Choose Paintbrush. • Stretch block vertically a little, as shown in illustration. • Move block slightly to the left. • Done.

5. Edit row graphic: • Choose Ink Swash. • Color, Graphic: 100% Magenta. • Move graphic to bottom of letterhead. • Stretch to fill space as shown. • Done.

6. Edit text block 2 (bottom block in layout): • Tab. • Resize block to fit above the newly moved row graphic. • Font: Stylus, Font Size: Medium. • Line Justify: Center, Placement: Top. • Style, Drop Shadow: Yes. • Colors, Behind Text: 100% Yellow. • Order: Send to Back. • Tab. • Type "You can count on us—we're the Professionals!," upper- and lowercase letters. • Tab. • Done.

7. Edit text block 1 (found in middle of project): • Tab. • Move text block to top of project. • Resize to fit beside square graphic at top, as shown in illustration. • Font: Stylus, Font Size: 40-point. • Line Justify: Center, Placement: Center.

• Tab. • Type "Professional Painters, Inc." on first line, upper- and lowercase letters. • Tab. • Font: New Zurica, Font Size: 14-point. • Tab. • Type business address and phone number on second line, upper- and lowercase letters. • Tab. • Done.

8. Select Add New Elements, add: • Text Block. Place block at bottom of letterhead. Remember to press Tab and Done after placing the element (you'll fill in the block in step 10).

9. Select Fill In or Edit.

10. Edit new text block: • Tab. • Resize block to fit across bottom, below row graphic. • Font: Signature, Font Size: Small. • Line Justify: Center, Placement: Bottom. • Colors, Behind Text: 100% Yellow. • Order: Send to Back. The color backgrounds for the bottom text blocks should overlap, forming a jagged rectangular shape, as shown in illustration. • Tab. • Type "over 75 years of experience," all lowercase letters. • Tab. • Done.

Memo/Business

Memos are fun and easy to make using the letterhead project type. You can design all kinds of memos for the office or school. Here's a stylistic memo designed from scratch, using an initial cap graphic (see Section 5). Follow these PSD-DOS steps.

1. Select: • Letterhead. • Create a New Project. • Regular.

2. Select **A**dd New Elements, add: • Square Graphic. • Two Text Blocks. • Ruled Line, Horizontal. • Place the square graphic in the upper left corner as shown in illustration. Place one text block beside graphic, the other text block below in an empty part of the project (you'll place it in step 5). Place the ruled line below the first text block, as shown in illustration. Remember to Tab and select **D**one after placing each element.

3. Select **F**ill In or Edit.

4. Edit square graphic: • Choose Other Libraries. • Choose Pattern from the initial cap graphic file (INITCAPS.PSG). • **S**cale block to fill space as shown in illustration. • **F**rame: Drop Shadow. • **C**olors, Graphic: 40% shade. • **D**one.

5. Edit text block 1 (placed in empty spot in project): • Tab. • **F**ont: Chaucer, Font **S**ize: 62-point. • Line Justify: Center, Placement: Top. • **C**olors, Text: 100% Blue. • **S**tyle, Drop Shadow: Yes. • Tab. • Type M, capital letter. • Tab. • **R**esize and **M**ove block so the letter M sits mostly inside the open white square of the initial cap graphic. • **D**one.

6. Edit text block 2 (beside square graphic at top): • Tab. • **R**esize block to fit beside initial cap graphic. • **F**ont: New Zurica Bold, Font **S**ize: 64-point. • Line **J**ustify: Full, Placement: Top. • **C**olors, Text: 100% Blue. • **S**tyle, Drop Shadow: Yes. • Tab. • Type EMO, all capital letters. • Tab. • **D**one.

7. Edit ruled line: • Choose Traditional. • **St**retch block across project below text block 2, as shown in illustration. • **D**one.

Design Tip You can also use the masthead you design for your letter or memo on envelopes, brochures, and flyers. You can even have a T-shirt shop transfer the pattern onto a shirt.

Notepad/School

Notepad projects make wonderful ways to communicate with a handwritten message. Or you can type your message right along with your design. But remember, these projects print two to a page, so try to economize! Here's a simple PSD-Windows notepad designed from scratch for school use.

1. Select: • Letterhead. • Notepad.

2. Select a Backdrop: • Choose Blank Page. • Click OK.

3. Select a Layout: • Choose No Layout. • Click OK.

4. Use the New Object tool or the **O**bject menu to add: • Row Graphic. • Headline Block. Place the row graphic at top. Place headline block at bottom.

5. Edit row graphic: • Double-click block. • Choose ABC 123. • Click OK.

6. Edit headline block: • Size block to fill space at bottom of project, as shown in example. • Double-click block. • **F**ont: DomCasual. • **S**hape: Bottom Arch. • **J**ustify: Center. • **C**ustomize: Effect 8. • Type "From the Desk of PRINCIPAL HUGHES," two lines, upper- and lowercase letters as shown (substitute your staff member's name). • Click OK.

Other Ideas   Remember, you can take your finished notepad design to a professional printer and have them put into actual notepads. This is a great office gift idea!

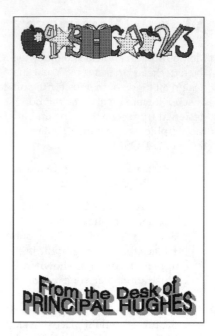

Your program does not have a notepad feature, but that shouldn't stop you from creating one anyway. Just design your letterhead project for the top of the page, then print it out. Have a professional printer create a notepad for you! Here's some simple steps for creating a school-oriented notepad:

1. Select: • Letterhead. • Design Your Own.

2. Select Graphic: • Choose Medium, Left. • Choose Graphics, Books.

3. Select Text: • You'll type in three lines and choose a different font and size. • First line, choose Small, Solid and type "A Note From." • Second line, choose Madera, Solid and type "PRINCIPAL." Press F5 to change size. • Third line, choose Madera, Solid and type "HUGHES." Press F5 to change size. • Each line should increase in point size so that the last line is the largest size. (Of course, you'll substitute your own principal's name.) • Press F8 to center in space.

Forms/Business

You can design all sorts of forms using the Print Shop programs; business forms, record-keeping forms, school report sheets, inventory forms, and much more. The following project shows an example of an invoice created on PSD-DOS.

1. Select: • Letterhead. • Create a New Project. • Regular.

2. Select a-Layout: • Choose Letterhead 12.

3. Select Fill In or Edit.

4. Edit square graphic: • Choose Tennis. • Move to the left as shown in illustration.

5. Edit ruled line: • Choose Scotch. • Done.

6. Edit text block: • Tab. • Font: New Zurica, Font Size: 12-point. • Line Justify: Left, Placement: Top. • Frame: Thick Line. • Tab. • Type in your company invoice information, use the Shift key and the hyphen key to make lines to write on. • Tab. • Done. • Depending upon how complicated your form is, this block may take some experimenting to create the look you want. In this example, the space bar was used to space out words, and the hyphen key was used to create lines.

7. Select Add New Elements, add: • Headline Block. • Text Block. Place the headline block at the top and the text block below the headline, as shown in illustration. Press Tab and Done when finished adding new elements.

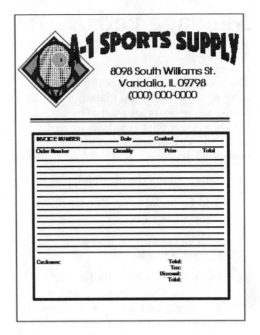

8. Select Fill In or Edit.

9. Edit headline: • Tab. • Resize block to stretch across top of project as shown in illustration. • Font: Boulder. • Shape: Top Arch. • Justify: Center. • Tab. • Type "A-1 SPORTS SUPPLY," all capital letters. • Tab. • Done.

10. Edit text block: • Tab. • Resize block to fit between headline block and ruled line block. • Font: Moderne, Font Size: Medium. • Line Justify: Center, Placement: Top. • Tab. • Type in company address and phone number, three lines, upper- and lowercase letters. • Tab. • Done.

Message Pads/ Home

The notepad orientation of the letter-head projects allow you to design numerous projects for written messages. Here's a clever PSD-Windows design idea to make a message pad to place by the phone at home.

1. Select: • Letterhead. • Notepad.

2. Select a Backdrop: • Choose Blank Page. • Click OK.

3. Select a Layout: • Choose No Layout. • Click OK.

4. Use the New Object tool or pull down the Object menu to add: • Two Square Graphics. • Headline Block. • Text Block. Place one square graphic in top half of project and resize to fill space. Place second graphic in lower left corner, resize to fill space as shown in illustration. Headline and text blocks will be rotated and placed in lower right corner.

5. Edit square graphic 1 (top): • Double-click block. • Choose Speech Bubble. • Click OK.

6. Edit square graphic 2 (bottom left corner): • Double-click block. • Choose Owl. • Click OK.

7. Edit headline block: • Enlarge block to fit headline, as shown in illustration. • Double-click block. • Font: Bazooka. • Shape: Rectangle. • Type "HEY!," all capital letters. • Click OK. • Rotate: 90 degrees. • You may have to resize to fit.

8. Edit text block: • Enlarge block to fit text, as shown in illustration. • Double-click block. • Font: New Zurica, Justification: Horizontal Center. • Type "THERE'S A MESSAGE FOR YOU," all capital letters. • Click OK. • Rotate: 90 degrees. • You may have to resize to fit.

Other Ideas   Design your own holiday message pads for home or office. You can also try making a holiday letterhead for correspondence with family and friends.

File Labels/ Business

Use the Print Shop programs to make labels for all kinds of uses: book labels, lunch box labels, gardening labels, food labels, envelope labels, and more. Follow the PSD-DOS steps in this project idea to make file labels for the office. By using the notepad orientation, you will be able to print out two sets of labels.

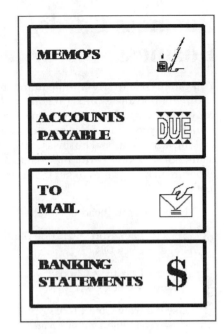

1. Select: • Letterhead. • Create a New Project. • Notepad.

2. Select Add New Elements, add: • Four Text Blocks. • Four Square Graphics. Place each text block in a row, taking up 1/4 of space, as shown in example. Each graphic should be placed inside text blocks on the far right side, as shown. Remember to press Tab and Done after placing each element.

3. Select Fill In or Edit.

4. Edit text block 1: • Tab. • Move block to top of project. • Resize to fill top 1/4 of area. • Font: Heather, Font Size: Medium. • Line Justify: Left, Placement: Center. • Frame: Thick Line. • Tab. • Type "MEMOS," all caps. • Tab. • Done.

5. Edit text block 2: • Tab. • Move block to top of project. • Resize to fill top 1/4 of area. • Font: Heather, Font Size: Medium. • Line Justify: Left, Placement: Center. • Frame: Thick Line. • Tab. • Type "ACCOUNTS PAYABLE," two lines, all caps. • Tab. • Done.

6. Edit text block 3: • Tab. • Move block to top of project. • Resize to fill top 1/4 of area. • Font: Heather, Font Size: Medium. • Line Justify: Left, Placement: Center. • Frame: Thick Line. • Tab. • Type "TO MAIL," two lines, all caps. • Tab. • Done.

7. Edit text block 4: • Tab. • Move block to top of project. • Resize to fill top 1/4 of area. • Font: Heather, Font Size: Medium. • Line Justify: Left, Placement: Center. • Frame: Thick Line. • Tab. • Type "BANKING STATEMENTS," two lines, all caps. • Tab. • Done.

8. Edit graphic block 1: • Choose Ink & Pen. • Done.

9. Edit graphic block 2: • Choose Other Libraries. • Choose calendar, Due. • Done.

10. Edit graphic block 3: • Choose Other Libraries. • Choose calendar, Mail. • Done.

11. Edit graphic block 4: • Choose Other Libraries. • Choose calendar, Money. • Done. Make sure all four labels are spaced so you can cut them out and use them.

Other Ideas   Follow similar steps to make nametags for parties, conventions, or club gatherings.

Business Cards/Business

You can make a nearly-infinite number of different business cards (in both conventional and large sizes) using the Print Shop programs. Here are steps for making a conventional business card using PSD-Windows. You may have to experiment a few times to get the size just right.

1. Select: • Letterhead. • Notepad.

2. Select a Backdrop: • Choose Blank Page. • Click OK.

3. Select a Layout: • Choose No Layout. • Click OK.

4. Use the New Object tool or pull down the Object menu to add: • Mini-Border. • Square Graphic. • Text Block. Place the text block in the middle of page, slightly to the right, size as shown in illustration. Place the square graphic to the left of the text block. Surround the text and graphic blocks with the mini-border, as shown. You'll want to scale your project to conventional business-card size. You may have to print this one or twice to find the correct size.

5. Edit mini-border: • Double-click block. • Choose Double Diamond. • Click OK.

6. Edit square graphic: • Double-click block. • Choose Happy Tooth. • Click OK.

7. Edit text block: • Double-click block. • Font: New Zurica, Size: 10-point, Justification: Horizontal Center. • Type business name, address, and phone number. • Use four lines, upper- and lowercase letters. Make first line of text bold. • Click OK.

You can create business cards using the letterhead or greeting-card project type. Just find a graphic you like, and add text with name, address, and phone number. Take your printout to a professional printer, and have him or her make a set of conventional business cards with your design!

Logos/Business

With the design capabilities available on your computer, you can create logos for use on letterheads, business cards, envelopes, brochures, flyers, newsletters, and more. Match a graphic with your company name, and experiment with different editing commands to combine the two elements. The following PSD-DOS steps show a logo at the top of a letterhead. Design elements (such as the ruled line) are used to keep the logo theme throughout the project.

1. Select: • Letterhead. • Create a New Project. • Regular.

2. Select Add New Elements, add: • Square Graphic. • Headline Block. • Two Ruled Lines, Horizontal. • Text Block. Place the headline at the very top of the project. Place the square graphic beneath the headline, slightly overlapping. Place one ruled line beneath the graphic block and the other near the bottom. Place the text block at the very bottom of the project. Size the elements as shown in example, and remember to press Tab and Done after placing each one.

3. Select Fill In or Edit.

4. Edit headline: • Font: New Zurica. • Shape: Top Arch. • Justify: Center. • Shadow: Drop Shadow. • Colors, Shadow: 100% Cyan. • Tab. • Type "Luv & Hugs Preschool," upper- and lowercase letters. • Tab. • Done.

5. Edit square graphic: • Choose Teddy. • Order: Send to Back. • Done.

6. Edit ruled line 1: • Choose Paper Links. • Order: Send to Back. Make sure the ruled line overlaps the square graphic slightly. • Done.

7. Edit ruled line 2: • Choose Paper Links. • Done.

8. Edit text block: • Tab. • Font: Paramount, Font Size: Medium. • Line Justify: Center, Placement: Center. • Tab. • Type business address and phone number, two lines, upper- and lowercase letters. • Tab. • Done.

Design Tip   To make a simple logo out of a headline and a square graphic, follow these steps:

1. Create two blocks, one a headline, the other a square graphic.

2. Experiment with layering the headline block over the graphic to make a logo.

Stationery

Signs & Flyers

Signs and flyers are useful in a variety of ways: announcing sales, new businesses, or special events, showing directions, identifying the lost and found, providing real estate notices, and more. Here are the basic steps for creating any sign or flyer using PSD. If you're using the Windows version, steps 8–11 will vary slightly.

1. Select Sign project from the Main menu screen.

2. Select Create a New project. (Not on PSD-Windows.)

3. Select the project's orientation.

4. Select a Backdrop.

5. Choose a graphic design.

6. Select a Layout.

7. Choose the layout design.

8. Select Fill In or Edit.

9. Fill in each layout element.

10. Save the project. Select Save from the menu list, and type in the file name.

11. Print the project. Select Print from the menu list. Choose the printer options, and select Print.

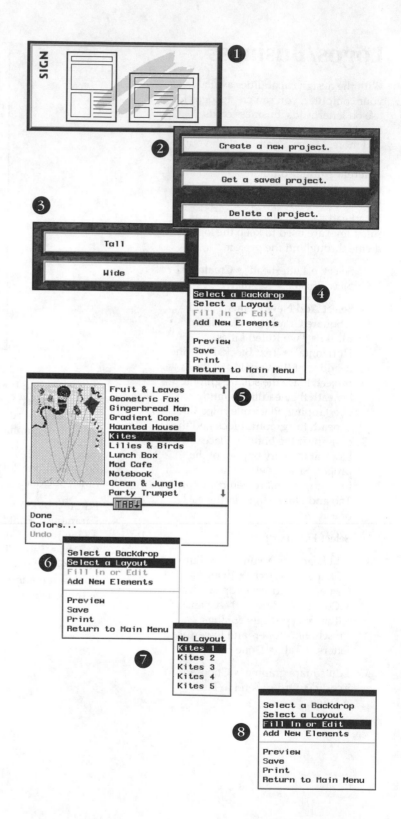

PSD-Windows Step 8 will look different on your screen. You'll use the Tool Palette and pull-down menus from the Menu bar to help you fill in each layout element. To follow steps 10 and 11, pull down the **F**ile menu to make selections to **S**ave and **P**rint.

You will find different steps to follow after step 3:

4. Select Border, and choose a border graphic if desired.

5. Select Graphic; choose a layout and art.

6. Select Message; choose a font and style; type in your text.

7. Select Save from the menu, and save your project.

8. Select Print from the menu to print your project.

Garage Sale/ Home

The following PSD-DOS project makes a great sign to post around the neighborhood, advertising a garage sale.

1. Select: • Sign. • Create a New Project. • Tall.

2. Select **A**dd New Elements; add:
    • **B**order. • **H**eadline. • **S**quare Graphic. • Six **T**ext Blocks. Place the headline at the top of the project. Place text block 1 below the headline. Text blocks 2–5 can be placed in the middle. Place text block 6 at bottom. Place square graphic in the middle, to be surrounded by rotated text blocks. Press Tab and **D**one after adding each element.

3. Select **F**ill In or Edit.

4. Edit border: • Choose Blue Check.
    • **D**one.

5. Edit headline: • Tab. • **F**ont: New Zurica. • **S**tyle: Blend Down.
    • **Sh**ape: Rectangle. • Line **J**ustify: Center. • Tab. • Type "GARAGE SALE!," all capital letters. • Tab.
    • **D**one.

6. Edit text block 1 (beneath headline): • Tab. • **F**ont: NewZuricaBold, Font **S**ize: Medium. • Line **J**ustify: Center, **P**lacement: Center. • Tab. • Type your address, upper- and lowercase letters. • Tab. • **D**one.

7. Edit square graphic (center of sign): • Choose Sale. • **D**one.
    • After placing tilted text blocks 2–5 as shown, you'll want to return to this graphic block and resize it to fill the space.

8. Edit text block 2: • Tab. • **F**ont: NewZuricaBold, Font **S**ize: 30-point. • Line **J**ustify: Center, **P**lacement: Center. • **S**tyle, Drop Shadow: Yes. • **R**otate 25 degrees.
    • **M**ove block and Resize to fill space. • Tab. • Type "BABY CLOTHES," two lines, all uppercase letters. • Tab. • **D**one.

9. Edit text block 3: • Repeat same actions as step 8 with the following changes • **R**otate 325 degrees.
    • **M**ove block as shown in example and Resize to fill space. • Tab.
    • Type "DISHES," all uppercase letters.

10. Edit text block 4: • Repeat same actions as step 8 with the following changes • **R**otate 325 degrees.
    • Type "APPLIANCES," all uppercase letters.

11. Edit text block 5: • Repeat same actions as step 8 with the following changes • **R**otate 25 degrees.
    • Type "FURNITURE," all uppercase letters.

12. Edit text block 6: • Tab. • **F**ont: Boulder, Font **S**ize: 42-point.
    • Line **J**ustify: Center, Placement: Center. • Tab. • Type date and time of garage sale, two lines, all capital letters. • **D**one.

Design Tip

Outdoor Sign Tip
If you're going to post your sign outdoors in inclement weather, be sure to laminate or cover the sign in clear plastic wrap to keep the ink from running. For sturdier signs, glue, staple, or tape the printout to heavy cardboard.

Promotional Sign/ Business

Promotional signs are an attractive way to bring attention to special items or services you have to offer. The following PSD-Windows sign project is for a restaurant.

1. Select: • **Sign**. • **Tall**.

2. Select a Backdrop: • Choose Mod Cafe. • Click OK.

3. Select a Layout: • Choose Mod Cafe 1. • Click OK.

4. Edit headline: • Double-click block. • **Font**: Jester. • Type "TODAY'S SPECIAL," all capital letters. • Click OK.

5. Edit text block 1: • Double-click block. • **Font**: Jester, **Size**: 30 point, **Justification**: Horizontal Center. • Type your restaurant's daily specials, 3 lines, upper- and lowercase letters. • Click OK.

6. Edit text block 2: • Double-click block. • **Font**: Palatia, **Style**: Bold on, **Size**: 30 point, **Justification**: Horizontal Center. • Type your restaurant's children's special (or other specials available), 4 lines, upper- and lowercase letters. • Underline first line if desired. • Click OK.

More Restaurant Graphics Try these other available restaurant-and-food-related graphics: Backdrop—Diner Food; Square graphics—Burger, Cherry Pie, Lunch, Restaurant; Row graphics—Orange Slices, Today's Special; Column graphics—Mod Cafe Cups, Restaurant Table, Waiter.

Here's a restaurant daily special sign you can try:

1. Select: • Sign or Poster. • Design Your Own. • Tall.

2. Select Border: • Choose Thin, Neon.

3. Select Graphic: • Choose Small Corners, Graphics, Picnic.

4. Select Message: • Choose Marin, Solid. • Type "TODAY'S SPECIAL," two lines, all capital letters. • Type your daily special, using Small font. • Press F8 to center. • Press F10 to preview.

Directional Sign/ School

The Print Shop programs are perfect for creating quick directional signs for special events. Here's a simple PSD-DOS idea for a school directional sign.

1. Select: • Sign. • Create a New Project. • Wide.

2. Select Add New Elements; add: • Border. • Headline. • Ruled Line, Horizontal. Place the headline in the center of the sign and the ruled line below. Size both elements as large as possible. Remember to select Tab and Done after adding each block.

3. Select Fill In or Edit.

4. Edit border: • Choose Diamond Corners. • Done.

5. Edit headline: • Tab. • Font: NewZuricaBold. • Shape: Rectangle. • Line Justify: Center. • Tab. • Type "REGISTRATION ROOM 25" (substitute your room number), two lines, all capital letters. • Tab. • Done.

6. Edit ruled line: • Choose Scotch. • Done.

PSD Windows Tip If you have other Windows graphic programs, you have another resource for art. You can create original artwork, or use clip art from other programs and paste them into your PSD projects. Simply copy the design from the other graphics program into the Windows Clipboard. Exit the program and go into PSD-Windows. Once you've opened the PSD project file you want, pull down the Edit menu and Paste the art into your project from the Clipboard. You'll then be able to scale, stretch, and modify it using PSD commands.

Help Wanted/ Business

Here's a handy project idea for posting a Help Wanted sign, whether it be in a window or on a bulletin board. Use these PSD-Windows steps to create this sign.

1. Select: • **Sign.** • **Wide.**

2. Select a Backdrop: • Choose Blank Page. • Click OK.

3. Select a Layout: • Choose Sign 13. • Click OK.

4. Edit border: • Double-click border frame. • Choose Autumn Leaves. • Click OK.

5. Edit headline: • Double-click block. • Font: Boulder, Style: Shadow on. • Justification: **Horizontal Center.** • Type "HELP WANTED," all capital letters. • Click OK.

6. Edit text block: • Double-click block. • Font: ParamountBold, Size: 50-point, • Justification: **Vertical bottom.** • Type brief hiring details. • Click OK.

HELP WANTED
Now Hiring Part-Time
Secretary
8-5, Mon-Fri
Some Evenings
APPLY WITHIN

Here's a similar help wanted sign you can create.

1. Select: • **Sign or Poster.** • **Design Your Own.** • **Wide.**

2. Select Border: • Choose Thin, Deco.

3. Select Message: • Choose Madera, Solid. • Type "HELP WANTED" and describe briefly the position you have open (use Sierra for description). • Press F8 to center. • Press F10 to preview.

Design Tip

Make your sign sturdier by attaching it to stiffer posterboard or cardboard.

Signs & Flyers

Lost & Found/ Home

The Print Shop programs can help you create a lost and found sign that's sure to be noticed. Try this PSD-DOS project.

1. Select: • Sign. • Create a New Project. • Tall.

2. Select a **Layout:** • Choose Sign 27.

3. Select **Fill In** or **Edit.**

4. Edit headline: • Tab. • Font: Boulder. • Shadow: Lower Right. • Tab. • Type "LOST," all capital letters. • Tab. • **Done.**

5. Edit square graphic: • Choose Lovable Pup. • Frame: Thick Line. • **Done.**

6. Edit text block: • Tab. • Font: Boulder, Font Size: 30-point. • Line Justify: Center, Placement: Center. • Tab. • Type a brief description of the missing pet, and the number to call. • Tab. • **Done.**

Lost & Found Sign for School   Here's a perfect sign for kids at school losing hats, scarves, and gloves. Create a tall sign using the Winter Child backdrop and layout 3. Headline should read "LOST & FOUND", and the text block should describe the lost item of the week.

Message Sign/ Home

Families on the go find it helpful to post reminder signs around the house for particular chores or errands, especially those that are repeated frequently. Here's a PSD-DOS project idea for creating a reminder message that can be hung on the refrigerator, posted on a door, or placed on a table.

1. Select: • Sign. • Create a New Project. • Wide.

2. Select a Layout: • Choose Sign 14.

3. Select Fill In or Edit.

4. Edit border: • Choose Geo. • Done.

5. Edit square graphic: • Choose Elephant Forgets. • Enlarge graphic slightly. • Done.

6. Edit text block: • Tab. • Font: Boulder, Font Size: Large. • Line Justify: Center, Placement: Center. • Tab. • Type "DON'T FORGET!" on one line, capital letters. • Tab. • Font: ParamountBold, Font Size: 46-point. • Tab. • Type message on next two lines, all capital letters. • Tab. • Done.

No Smoking Sign for Office   Create a simple, effective no smoking sign using the No Smoking square graphic, or making your own with the International No square graphic.

1. Create a wide sign; use the Film Loop border.

2. Add a text block to fill the inside space, select Boulder typestyle and type "SMOKING".

3. Add the International No square graphic, and resize to fit over the text block.

4. Edit the Colors of the graphic, and shade at 50% Red.

5. Edit the Order and choose Send to Back.

The following steps will let you create a reminder message for soccer practice.

1. Select: • Sign or Poster. • Design Your Own. • Wide.

2. Select Border: • Choose Thin, Blocks.

3. Select Graphic: • Choose Small Pair, Graphics, Soccer.

4. Select Message: • Choose Madera, Solid. • Type "SOCCER PRAC-TICE" tonight at 6! • Press F8 to center. • Press F10 to preview.

Signs & Flyers

New Business Flyer/Business

Flyers are always a good way to market a new business. The following PSD-DOS project idea is for a Grand Opening flyer for a travel agency; it can be distributed on car windshields, bulletin boards, mailboxes, and more.

1. Select: • Sign. • Create a New Project. • Tall.

2. Select a **B**ackdrop: • Choose Coastal Scene. • **D**one.

3. Select a **L**ayout: • Choose Sign 5.

4. Select **A**dd New Elements; add: • Two additional **T**ext Blocks. Place one block directly below headline, and the second block in bottom left corner. Both blocks should be somewhat small. Remember to press Tab and **D**one after adding each element.

5. Select Fill In or Edit.

6. Edit headline: • Tab. • **F**ont: PalatiaBold. • **S**hadow: Shape Shadow. • **S**hape: Arc Up. • **C**olors, Text: White, Shadow: Black, Behind Text: Clear. • Tab. • Type "Travis Travel Agency" (or name of your company), upper- and lowercase letters. • Tab. • **D**one.

7. Edit text block 1 (newly-added small block directly below headline): • Tab. • **F**ont: New Zurica, Font **S**ize: X-small. • Line **J**ustify: Center, Placement: Top. • Tab. • Type name of owners (as shown in example), upper- and lowercase letters. • Tab. • **F**ont: Signature, Font **S**ize: X-small. • Tab. • Type years of experience, two lines, upper- and lowercase letters. • Tab. • **D**one.

8. Edit text block 2 (large block in middle of sign): • Tab. • **F**ont: Jester, Font **S**ize: 28-point. • Line **J**ustify: Center, Placement: Center. • **F**rame: Thin Line. • Resize block to fit beside palm tree. • Tab. • Type "GRAND OPENING! Stop in for a Visit! Register to Win a Trip to Hawaii!", six lines, upper- and lowercase letters as shown. • Tab. • **D**one.

9. Edit text block 3: • Tab. • **F**ont: Moderne, Font **S**ize: Small. • Line **J**ustify: Center, Placement: Center. • **F**rame: Drop Shadow. • **M**ove block to lower right corner. • Tab. • Type "Let us help you plan your dream vacation!", four lines, upper- and lowercase letters. • Tab. • **D**one.

10. Edit text block 4 (created in step 4): • Tab. • **F**ont: Boulder, Font **S**ize: Small. • Line **J**ustify: Center, Placement: Top. • Tab. • Type in address of new business, and the phone number. • Tab. • **D**one.

Design Tip

Copy your flyers onto colored paper for greater impact. You can also use a vertical tri-fold on your flyer, to turn it into an instant mailer! The blank side of the flyer should appear on the outside. Just staple or tape it closed, and add an address!

Sale Flyer/School

Flyers can be used to promote sales for businesses, neighborhoods, and more. The PSD-Windows project below is an example of a school sale flyer.

1. Select: • **Sign**. • **Tall**.

2. Select a Backdrop: • Choose Gingerbread Man. • Click OK.

3. Select a Layout: • Choose Gingerbread Man 5. • Click OK.

4. Edit headline: • Double-click block. • Font: Boulder. • Customize, Effect: Drop Shadow, Position: Lower Right. • Type "BAKE SALE", all capital letters. • Click OK.

5. Edit text block 1 (below headline): • Double-click block. • Font: Moderne, Size: 28-point, Justification: Horizontal Center. • Type details about sale (date, time, and place), six lines as shown in example, upper- and lowercase letters. • Choose X-small size for last two lines. • Click OK. • With the Frame tool, choose No Frame.

6. Edit text block 2: • Move block to fit beside gingerbread man. • Double-click block. • Font: Boulder, Size: 28-point, Justification: Horizontal Center. • Type "PIES! CAKES! COOKIES! BREADS! BROWNIES! And More!," five lines, upper- and lowercase letters as shown. • Click OK. • From the color palette, select Yellow for behind the text.

7. Use the New Object tool or pull down the **O**bject menu to add: • **T**ext block. Place block in bottom right corner, as shown in example.

8. Edit new text block: • Double-click block. • Font: Boulder, Size: Small, Justification: Horizontal Center. • Type phone number to be called. • Click OK. • From the color palette, choose white for text and black for behind text.

Color Tip Have the kids in your school help color the signs with crayons, markers, or paint!

Real Estate Signs/ Home

Sale signs for the home can be used in a variety of ways, selling cars, lawn equipment, or even real estate. The PSD-Windows project idea below is for a sign that can be posted in a yard, or in a window.

1. Select: • **Sign.** • **Wide.**

2. Select a Backdrop: • Choose Blank Page. • Click OK.

3. Select a Layout: • Choose Sign 13. • Click OK.

4. Edit border: • Double-click border frame. • Choose Diamond Corners. • Click OK.

5. Edit headline: • Click block. • Use the Delete tool to delete the headline block.

6. Use the New Object tool or pull down the **O**bject menu to add: • **Text Block.** Size the block to fill top of sign, as shown in example.

7. Edit new text block: • Double-click block. • **Font:** Boulder, **Size:** 125-point, Justification: **H**orizontal Center. • Type "FOR SALE," all capital letters. • Click OK. • From the color palette, choose White for text and Black for behind text.

8. Edit text block (bottom block): • Double-click block. • **Font:** Boulder, **Size:** Large, Justification: **H**orizontal Center. • Type "BY OWNER call 000-0000," three lines, upper- and lowercase letters. • Click OK.

Outdoor Sign Tip Be sure to mount your sign onto sturdier cardboard or posterboard. If the weather is damp or rainy, laminate or wrap your sign in plastic to keep the ink from running.

The following steps will let you create a reminder message for soccer practice.

1. Select: • Sign or Poster. • Design Your Own. • Wide.

2. Select Border: • Choose Thin, Double Line.

3. Select Message: • Choose Amador, Solid. • Type "FOR SALE by Owner" and add the phone number. • Press F8 to Center. • Press F10 to preview.

Event Flyer/School

You can create event flyers for home, school, community, or office. Follow these PSD-DOS steps to make an event flyer for school.

1. Select: • Sign. • Create a New Project. • Tall.

2. Select a **Backdrop:** • Choose Football Field. • **Done.**

3. Select a **Layout:** • Choose layout 3.

4. Select **Fill In** or Edit.

5. Edit text block: • **Tab.** • Resize block to make room for headline at top. • **Font:** Jester, **Font Size:** 26-point. • **Line Justify:** Center, **Placement:** Center. • **Tab.** • Type event message, date, and time, five lines, upper- and lowercase letters. • **Tab.** • **Done.**

6. Edit bottom headline block: • **Tab.** • Resize block as large as possible across bottom of sign. • **Shadow:** Drop Shadow. • **Shape:** Pennant Right. • **Font:** Bazooka. • **Line Justify:** Center. • **Colors, Text:** Black, **Shadow:** Grey. • **Tab.** • Type your team's name, all capital letters. • **Tab.** • **Done.**

7. Select **Add New Elements;** add: • **Headline.** Place at top of sign. Select **Tab** and **Done.**

8. Select **Fill In** or Edit.

9. Edit new headline block: • **Tab.** • Resize as large as possible. • **Font:** Boulder. • **Line Justify:** Center. • **Shadow:** Drop Shadow. • **Shape:** Double Arch Up. • **Colors, Shadow:** Grey. • **Tab.** • Type "TEAM RALLY!", all capital letters. • **Tab.** • **Done.**

Community Event Flyers You'll be able to make all sorts of flyers for special activities around your town. Here's an idea for Halloween pumpkin-carving contest:

1. Select a tall sign, layout 13.

2. Use the Jolly Pumpkins row graphics at the top and bottom.

3. Type the event details in Jester, 30-point. Resize the text block to make room for a column graphic on the right.

4. Add a column graphic, Halloween Candy.

Signs & Flyers

Political-Election Flyers/Community

Whether it be an election at school, your neighborhood, or community, signs can help your campaign. Here's a simple PSD-DOS election sign idea.

1. Select: • Sign. • Create a New Project. • Tall.

2. Select a Layout: • Choose Sign 19.

3. Select Fill In or Edit.

4. Edit border: • Choose Stars & Stripes. • Done.

5. Edit headline: • Tab. • Font: Boulder. • Line Justify: Center. • Shadow: Block Shadow. • Colors, Shadow: Grey. • Tab. • Type "VOTE", all capital letters. • Tab. • Done.

6. Edit text block: • Tab. • Font: Tubular, Font Size: 120-point. • Line Justify: Center, Placement: Center. • Style, Drop Shadow: Yes. • Tab. • Type your candidate's name, two lines, all capital letters. • Tab. • Font: StageCoach, Font Size: 44-point. • Tab. • Type the office they're running for, one line, upper- and lowercase letters. • Tab. • Done.

You can make a very simple election sign using The New Print Shop.

1. Select: • Sign or Poster. • Design Your Own. • Tall.

2. Select Border: • Choose Thin, Neon.

3. Select Message: • Choose Amador, Raised. • Type "VOTE" on one line. • Type the name of your candidate on the next two lines (Madera, Solid). • Type the running position on the bottom line (Sutter, Solid). • Press F8 to center.

Door Signs/Home

Here's a PSD-Windows idea for a door sign for a child's room. The Print Shop programs allow you to create numerous sign ideas to post on doors at home, at school, or in the office.

1. Select: • **Sign.** • **Tall.**

2. Select a Backdrop: • Choose Volcano. • Click OK.

3. Select a Layout: • Choose Volcano 5. • Click OK.

4. Edit text block: • Double-click block. • Font: Boulder, Size: Large, Justification: Horizontal Full.
   • Type "DANGER!", capital letters.
   • Font: Bazooka, Size: Medium.
   • Type "ROOM MAY EXPLODE!", capital letters. • Click OK.

5. Edit headline: • Double-click block.
   • Font: Subway. • Justification: Horizontal Right. • Type "KEEP OUT!", two lines, all capital letters.
   • Click OK.

Here's another version of a teenager's door sign.

1. Select: • Sign or Poster. • Design Your Own. • Tall.

2. Select Graphic: • Choose Full Panel, Jukebox.

3. Select Message: • Choose Madera, Solid. • Type "WARNING" on the top line. • Type "LOUD MUSIC INSIDE", on the bottom three lines (Sierra, Solid). • Press F8 to center.

Science Fair Signage/School

Help make your child's science-fair project a big success with easy-to-read signs, created with the Print Shop programs. Follow these PSD-DOS steps:

1. Select: • Sign. • Create a New Project. • Wide.

2. Select a Layout: • Choose Sign 2.

3. Select Fill In or Edit.

4. Edit headline: • Tab. • Font: New Zurica, Line Justify: Full. • Shadow: Block Shadow. • Tab. • Type science project's title, all capital letters. • Tab. • Done.

5. Edit text block 1: • Tab. • Font: Tribune, Font Size: Medium. • Line Justify: Left, Placement: Top. • Tab. • Type a brief introduction to your project, upper- and lowercase letters. • Tab. • Done.

6. Edit text block 2: • Tab. • Font: Tribune, Font Size: 30-point. • Line Justify: Right, Placement: Top. • Colors, Behind Text: 100% Cyan. • Tab. • Type your project information, upper- and lowercase letters. • Tab. • Done.

7. Edit square graphics: • Choose World. • Apply to All: Yes. Choose the same graphic for all four blocks. • Done.

Here's another version of a science fair sign. The project focuses on sports.

1. Select: • Sign or Poster. • Design Your Own. • Wide.

2. Select Graphic: • Choose Small Corners. • Choose Graphics, Baseball, Basketball, Football, Soccer, one for each corner graphic.

3. Select Message: • Choose Madera, Solid. • Type "THE EFFECTS OF SPORTS ON THE HUMAN BODY." • Press F8 to center.

Banners

For those occasions requiring a really big sign, banner projects are just the thing. Banners are simple to create, print and hang. They come in handy for party decorations, big sale events, science fair projects, team rallies, and much more. With the Print Shop programs, you'll be able to create horizontal banners and vertical banners. Here are the basic steps for creating any banner using PSD. If you're using the Windows version, steps 8–11 will vary slightly.

1. Select Banner project from the Main menu screen.

2. Select Create a New Project. (Not in PSD-Windows.)

3. Select project orientation.

4. Select a Backdrop.

5. Choose a graphic design.

6. Select a Layout.

7. Choose a layout design.

8. Select Fill In or Edit.

9. Fill in each layout element.

10. Save the project. Select Save from the menu list, and type in the file name.

11. Print the project. Select Print from the menu list. Choose the printer options and select Print.

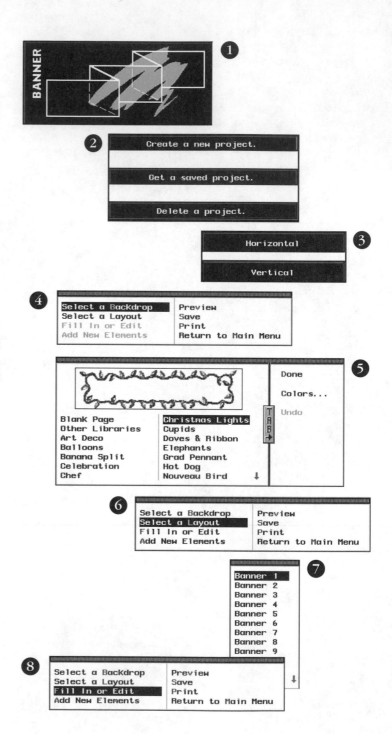

When creating banner projects, there are a few things to remember. Banners are made to be big. That means there isn't much room for lots of text and graphics. Banner text works a lot like headline blocks; horizontal banners can have up to two lines of text, and vertical banners can have one line of text. (There are ways to get around this rule! See the Design Tip on the election banner project page.) But unlike headlines, banner text does not get squeezed to fit into the space. Instead, the more letters and words you type, the longer the banner.

If you're using PSD, you can also increase banner length using the Adjust Length option from the Edit menu; Leading Space can add inches to the front end of your banner, Trailing Space can add inches to the back end of your banner.

Since banners are so big, you won't always be able to see the whole project on your screen. Use the scrolling functions to view the different parts of your banner. (If you're using PSD, use the + or – keys on your keyboard's numeric keypad to scroll. If you're using NPS, use the F10 key and the Enter key to scroll.)

If you have PSD release 1.2, your banners will now print more smoothly. Plus, two new features are added to your options. You can now see where the page breaks are, and you can manually set the number of banner pages you want your project to be.

PSD-Windows Step 8 will look different on your screen. You'll use the Tool Palette and pull-down menus from the Menu bar to help you fill in each layout element. To follow steps 10 and 11, pull down the File menu to make selections.

You will find different steps to follow after step 3:

4. Select Graphic and choose a graphic if desired.

5. Select Message; choose a font and style, and type in the text.

6. Select Trim (a border on two sides of project), and choose a trim if desired.

7. Select Save from the menu, and save your project.

8. Select Print from the menu to print your project.

Banners

Garage Sale/ Home

A big banner can draw a lot of attention to a neighborhood sale. The following PSD-DOS project idea will help you create a simple, yet attractive, garage sale banner.

1. Select: • Banner. • Create a New Project. • Horizontal.

2. Select a Layout: • Choose Banner 28.

3. Select Add New Elements, add: • Border. Press Tab and Done when finished adding element.

4. Select Fill In or Edit.

5. Edit border: • Choose Blue Check. • Done.

6. Edit headline: • Tab. • Font: Boulder. • Shadow: Drop Shadow, Lower Right. • Line Justify: Center. • Tab. • Type "GARAGE SALE", all capital letters. • Done.

7. Edit graphic block: • Tab. • Delete graphic block. • Done.

8. Select Add New Elements, add: • Text Block. Place block at bottom of banner. Remember to select Tab and Done after placing element.

9. Select Fill In or Edit.

10. Edit new text block: • Tab. • Resize block to fill bottom of banner. • Font: ParamountBold, Font Size: Small. • Line Justify: Full, Placement: Center. • Tab. • Type the dates and times of the garage sale, all capital letters. • Tab. • Done.

![GARAGE SALE FRI & SAT 9-5 banner]

Banner Tip If you're using string or wire to hang your banner, it's a good idea to reinforce the banner in the corners from which it will hang. This is especially true for banners displayed outside on windy days. Before punching holes for the string or wire, try reinforcing the back of the banner with heavy-duty tape. Another idea is adding weights to the bottom of the banner to keep it from flapping.

You can create a garage sale sign similar to the one shown, but with graphics. Follow these steps:

1. Select: • Banner. • Design Your Own. • Horizontal.

2. Select Graphic: • Choose Full Panel on Both Ends. • Choose Saletag.

3. Select Message: • Choose Large Line over Small. • Madera, Solid. • Type "GARAGE SALE Fri & Sat 9–5", two lines.

4. Select Trim: • Thin. • Choose Frilly.

5. Select Preview to see what the project will look like.

Election/Community

Banners are great for political campaigning, whether it be a school, local or national election. Here's a PSD-DOS idea for a patriotic-looking banner.

1. Select: • Banner. • Create a New Project. • Horizontal.

2. Select a-Layout: • Choose Banner 2.

3. Select Fill In or Edit.

4. Edit border: • Choose Stars & Stripes. • Done.

5. Edit square graphics: • Choose Other Libraries. • Choose calendar, Flag for both graphic blocks. • Done.

6. Edit headline: • Tab. • Font: Boulder, Font Size: Large/Small. • Shadow: Drop Shadow. • Tab. • Type the name of the person running for election, and what position they're running for, all capital letters. • Tab. • Done.

While you won't be able to duplicate the project shown here, follow these instructions for an election banner with a slogan.

1. Select: • Banner. • Design Your Own. • Horizontal.

2. Select Graphic: • Choose Large Graphic on Both Ends. • Choose Graphics, Ribbon.

3. Select Message: • Choose Small Line over Large. • Select Amador, Raised. • Type "ELECT A REAL WINNER" on the first line, all capital letters. • Type your candidate's name on the second line, upper and lowercase letters.

4. Select Trim: • Thin. • Choose Ribbon.

5. Select Preview to see what the project will look like.

Design Tip

Need more than two lines of text in your horizontal banner? Modify your banner layout to include a text block that fits another line.

Sports/School

What better way to root for your school's team or favorite sports star than with a large banner! Banners can be draped inside gymnasiums and school hallways, waved from bleacher stands, or taped to team buses, lockers, and more. The PSD-Windows project idea on this page illustrates how to create a vertical banner.

1. Select: • Banner. • Vertical.

2. Select a Backdrop: • Choose Blank Page. • Click OK.

3. Select a Layout: • Choose Banner 3. • Click OK.

4. Edit headline: • Double-click block. • Font: Tribune, Style: Bold on, Shadow on. • Type your team's name, all capital letters. • Click OK.

5. Edit column graphic: • Double-click block. • Choose Football Player. • Click OK.

6. Select a Backdrop: • Choose Playing Field. • Click OK.

Banner Flags and Pennants   You can cut out or trim banner projects to make flags or pennants. Just attach your banner to a lightweight balsa stick or wooden rod—and wave it to cheer on your favorite team!

Here's a vertical team banner for basketball.

1. Select: • Banner. • Design Your Own. • Vertical.

2. Select Graphic: • Choose Large Graphic Both Ends. • Choose Graphics, Basketball.

3. Select Message: • Select Sutter, Solid. • Type your team's name, all capital letters.

4. Select Trim: • Thin. • Choose Double Line.

5. Select Preview to see what the project will look like.

Party/Home

Large banners make excellent party decorations for home, school, or business. Follow these PSD-DOS steps to create a simple birthday banner.

1. Select: • Banner. • Create a New Project. • Horizontal.

2. Select a-Layout: • Choose Banner 22.

3. Select Fill In or Edit.

4. Edit headline: • Tab. • Font: New Zurica, Shadow: Drop Shadow, Lower Right. • Tab. • Type "HAPPY BIRTHDAY!", two lines, all capital letters. • Tab. • Done.

5. Edit square graphic blocks: • Choose Birthday Cake for both square graphics. • Done.

6. Edit row graphic: • Tab. • Delete row graphic. • Done.

7. Select Add New Elements; add: • Text Block. Place block below headline and size to fill remaining space, as shown in illustration. Remember to Tab and select Done after placing element.

8. Edit new text block: • Tab. • Font: Paramount, Font Size: Small. • Line Justify: Full, Placement: Center. • Type the name of the birthday person, all capital letters. • Tab. • Done.

Make a 3-D Banner   To give added punch to your party banners, attach extra graphics, streamers, or balloons. To add 3-D graphics, follow these steps:

1. Print out extra copies of graphics (such as the Firecracker square graphic) to use on your banner.

2. Cut out the shape of the graphic.

3. Take a narrow strip of paper and fold it accordion-style.

4. Attach the graphic shape to one end of the strip. Attach the other end of the strip to the banner. Try using different lengths of paper strips to create your 3-D art. Once all your 3-D graphics are attached, you should have a banner with art that springs off!

You won't be able to duplicate the idea shown, but try these steps for a snazzy birthday banner.

1. Select: • Banner. • Design Your Own. • Horizontal.

2. Select Graphic: • Choose Large Graphic Both Ends. • Choose Graphics, Party Favor.

3. Select Message: • Choose Two Equal Lines. • Select Marin, Solid. • Type "HAPPY BIRTHDAY" on the first line, all capital letters. • Type the name of the birthday person on the second line, all capital letters.

4. Select Trim: • Thin. • Choose Neon.

5. Select Preview to see what the project will look like.

Store Sale/Business

Use banners to advertise new store items, sales, services, and more. This PSD-Windows project idea makes an ideal sale sign for your business.

1. Select: • Banner. • Horizontal.

2. Select a Backdrop: • Choose Blank Page. • Click OK.

3. Select a Layout: • Choose Banner 1. • Click OK.

4. Edit border: • Double-click border frame. • Choose Triangle. • Click OK.

5. Edit headline: • Double-click block. • Font: Subway, Size: Large/Small. • Type your sales feature, all capital letters, two lines. • Click OK.

6. Edit square graphic block 1 (left): • Double-click block. • Choose Sale. • Click OK. • Rotate block as shown in example (25 degrees). • Scale block to fill space between text and border.

7. Edit square graphic block 2 (right): • Double-click block. • Choose Sale. • Click OK. • Rotate block as shown in example (325 degrees). • Scale block to fill space between text and border.

Other Project Ideas   Is your school, church, or club having a fund-raiser? Use banners to advertise and decorate. Layouts like Number 11 make great use of art, border, and text.

Here's an alternative sale banner idea you can try on NPS.

1. Select: • Banner. • Design Your Own. • Horizontal.

2. Select Graphic: • Choose Full Panel on Both Ends. • Choose Saletag.

3. Select Message: • Choose Two Equal Lines. • Select Madera, Solid. • Type your sales feature, two lines.

4. Select Trim: • Thin. • Choose Frilly.

5. Select Preview to see what the project will look like.

Design Tip

Need a sturdier banner? Attach your banner projects to posterboard or other stiff cardboard products to add plenty of support.

Science Fair/School

Banners can be used to make signage for school fairs and exhibits. The following PSD-Windows example is a simple banner for a science-fair project. The Chef backdrop is perfect for a science project in which something is made by following steps like those in a recipe. Additional banners can demonstrate the various steps involved with the project, and its results.

1. Select: • Banner. • Horizontal.

2. Select a Backdrop: • Choose Chef. • Click OK.

3. Select a Layout: • Choose Chef 2. • Click OK.

4. Edit headline: • Double-click block. • Font: Jester. • Type your banner project's title, two lines, all capital letters. • Click OK.

Other Banner Ideas   Use Print Shop banners for professional trade shows and business presentations. With the crisp graphics and text, you can create quality banners that are sure to draw attention to your booth!

Try these NPS steps to create a science fair banner you can use with ease!

1. Select: •Banner. •Design Your Own. •Horizontal.

2. Select Graphic: •Choose Large Graphic Both Ends. •Choose Mushrooms from the Sampler Edition (an extra graphics collection for the NPS).

3. Select Message: •Choose Two Equal Lines. •Select Amador, solid. •Type same message as shown in example above.

4. Select Trim: •Thin. •Choose Ribbon.

5. Select Preview to see what the project will look like.

Design Tip
Print your banner on colored paper for even greater eye-catching appeal!

Finish Line/ Community

If your community, school, or business is sponsoring a marathon or fun-run race, you'll need a finish line. Banners make excellent finish lines! Try this PSD-DOS project idea to create a simple finish line.

1. Select: • Banner. • Create a New Project. • Horizontal.

2. Select a Layout: • Choose Banner 13.

3. Select Fill In or Edit.

4. Edit border: • Select Stars & Stripes. • **Done**.

5. Edit headline: • *Do not edit this block*. You'll replace this headline block with a text block in step 6.

6. Select Add New Elements; add: • Text Block. Size block to fill entire space inside border. Press Tab and **D**one when finished adding element.

7. Select Fill In or Edit.

8. Edit text block: • Tab. • Font: Subway, Font Size: Medium. • Line Justify: Full, Placement: Center. • Tab. • Type "FINISH LINE", all capital letters. • Tab. • **D**one.

Other Finish-Line Ideas   You can use your banner to hang above the finish line, or you can have the winner break through the banner as they cross the finish line!

Design Tip

To make longer finish-line banners, don't forget to use the Adjust Length commands to add inches to the front and back ends of your banner project.

Contest Event/ Community

Use the Print Shop programs to create great banners for community, school, or business contests. The project idea shown here is for a pie-eating contest at a community fair. Follow these PSD-DOS steps.

1. Select: • Banner. • Create a New Project. • Horizontal.

2. Select a **B**ackdrop: • Choose Art Deco. • **D**one.

3. Select a **L**ayout: • Choose Art Deco 5.

4. Select **F**ill In or Edit.

5. Edit graphic block: • Select Cherry Pie. • Stretch block to fill space on left side of banner. • **D**one.

6. Edit headline: • Tab. • **F**ont: Boulder, Font Size: Small/Large. • Shadow: Block Shadow. • Tab. • Type "PIE-EATING CONTEST", two lines, capital letters. • Tab. • **D**one.

Other Banner Ideas   Contest banners can be used at schools, businesses, and more. Here are some other contest banner ideas: spelling bee, game booths for the school fair, sales contests at the office, prize giveaways to bring in customers, birthday parties, family reunion and picnic activities, and athletic events.

You can create a similar banner following these NPS steps:

1. Select: • Banner. • Design Your Own. • Horizontal.

2. Select Graphic: • Large Graphic Both Ends. • Choose Cake Slice. (You may even wish to use the Graphic Editor option from the main menu to change the cake slice to look more like a pie slice.)

3. Select Message: • Choose Small Line over Large. • Select Madera, Raised. • Type "Pie Eating Contest", all capital letters as shown in illustration.

4. Select Trim: • Thin. • Choose Maze.

5. Select Preview to see what banner will look like.

Banners

Calendars

With the versatile Print Shop calendars, you can make numerous projects for your home, office, school, or community. Create your own yearly, monthly, weekly, or daily calendars to keep for yourself or give away. Here are the basic steps for creating any calendar using PSD. If you're using the Windows version, steps 10–13 will vary slightly.

1. Select Calendar project from the Main menu screen.

2. Select Create a New Project. (Not on PSD-Windows.)

3. Select the project orientation.

4. Select the calendar type (yearly, monthly, weekly, daily).

5. Select the calendar year. If you've chosen a monthly, weekly, or daily calendar, more menus will appear to narrow down the details, such as which exact month, week, or times. Make the appropriate selections when prompted.

6. Select a Backdrop from the menu list, if you want.

7. Select a backdrop graphic, if you want.

8. Select a Layout from the menu list.

9. Choose a layout design.

10. Select Fill In or Edit.

11. Fill in each layout element.

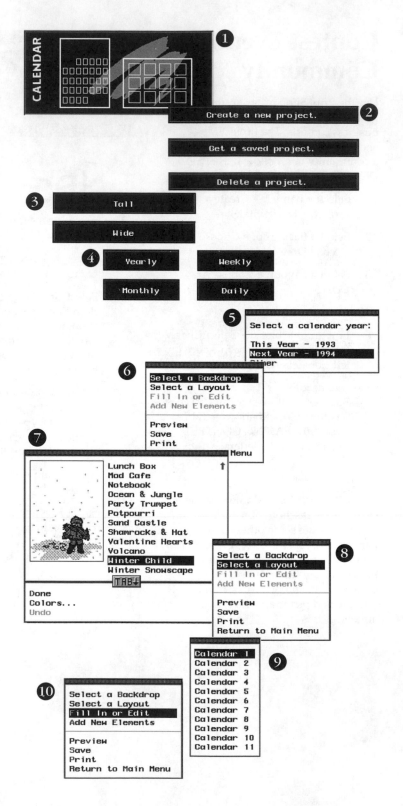

12. Save the project. Select Save from the menu list, and type in file name.

13. Print project. Select Print from the menu list. Choose printer options, and select Print.

When working with calendar projects, you will always be required to choose a layout as you begin your project. You can modify headline, graphics, and text blocks, but the calendar block itself has limited editing commands, unless you are using PSD version 1.2. For example, you will not be able to reposition or scale a calendar block as you can with other layout elements. However, if you're using version 1.2, you can.

With PSD version 1.2, several new calendar features have been added. You can use the Language option to print your calendar in one of five languages, there are more hours added to the daily calendar, and you can now mark Sundays in red for yearly or monthly calendars. You can also edit the last days of the month in a monthly calendar with version 1.2.

With all PSD programs, each calendar project automatically assigns a year, month, or week title as a headline or text block. For example, when creating a yearly calendar, PSD automatically will display the year you've chosen. You can modify these blocks at any time, but they're handy to use as is and can save you a step in designing your calendar.

The only editing command that differs from other commands you've been using is the Style command for a yearly calendar project. Instead of text or graphic styles, this menu lists three types of calendar styles: *Plain, Lines,* or *Boxes.* All of these affect how the twelve months of the year are displayed. Plain displays the months without any frills.

Lines will add lines under the names of the months. Boxes will place individual boxes around each month.

Calendar graphics, as described in Section 5, make wonderful enhancements for any calendar project. You can also use square, row, and column graphics to help illustrate your calendar designs.

PSD-Windows Step 10 will look different on your screen. You'll use the Tool Palette and pull-down menus from the Menu bar to help you fill in each layout element. To follow steps 12 and 13, pull down the File menu to make selections.

You won't be able to select a project orientation as in step 3. Your calendar projects will always be tall, not wide. You will also find different steps to follow after step 5:

6. Select Graphic, and choose a graphic and layout if you want.

7. Select Message, and choose a font, style, and type in text (year, month, date will automatically display depending upon what type of calendar project you've chosen).

8. Select Ruled Line, if you want.

9. Select Middle of Calendar, and edit your calendar project with your own dates and graphics.

10. Repeat steps 6–8 to design the bottom of your calendar, if you want.

11. Select Save from the menu, and save your project.

12. Select Print from the menu to print your project.

Yearly/Office

Yearly calendars are always useful around the home, office, or school. This PSD-DOS idea is a perfect project for advertising your company or business. Follow these steps to create a yearly calendar that can be given to customers, clients, associates, and others. By adding your company name, address, and phone number to a yearly calendar, you've created instant advertising! Have the calendars printed on quality paper in large quantities at your local printing store.

1. Select: • Calendar. • Create a New Project. • Tall. • Calendar type. • Calendar year.

2. Select a **Backdrop:** • Choose Ocean & Jungle. • **Done.**

3. Select a **Layout:** • Choose Ocean & Jungle 2.

4. Select **F**ill In or Edit.

5. Edit calendar block: • **Style:** Lines. • **Font:** New Zurica. • **Done.**

6. Edit headline: • Tab. • **Font:** NewZuricaBold. • **Colors:** Magenta. • Tab. • Type your company name, upper- and lowercase letters. • Tab. • **Done.**

7. Select **A**dd New Elements, add: • Two Text Blocks. Place one text block at top underneath headline. Place other block at very bottom for year. Press Tab and **D**one after placing each element.

8. Select **F**ill In or Edit.

9. Edit bottom text block: • Tab. • **Font:** Boulder, **Font Size:** 50-point. • Line **J**ustify: Center, **P**lacement: Center. • Tab. • Type year. • Tab. • **Done.**

10. Edit top text block (beneath headline): • Tab. • Resize block to fit below headline in space between headline and calendar block. • **Font:** Boulder, **Font Size:** X-small. • Line **J**ustify: Center, **P**lacement: Center. • Tab. • Type company phone number on first line. • Tab. • **Font:** New Zurica, **Font Size:** 10-point. • Tab. • Type company address on second line, upper- and lowercase letters. • Tab. • **Done.**

Design Tip

Try using a large graphic layered behind your calendar block, shaded at 30% or 40%. This creates a nice screened background to your calendar design. Be sure to choose bold fonts or thick lines to place on top of shaded art.

Monthly/Home

If you're having trouble keeping up with family schedules, try this PSD-DOS idea for a monthly calendar.

1. Select: • Calendar. • Create a New Project. • Wide. • Calendar type. • Calendar year. • Month.

2. Select a Layout: • Choose Calendar 5.

3. Select Fill In or Edit.

4. Edit calendar block: • Font: New Zurica. • Done.

5. Edit headline: • Tab. • Shape: Round Top. • Done.

6. Edit column graphic block: • Choose Bat & Gloves. • Shadow: Drop Shadow. • Done.

7. Select Add New Elements, add: • Row Graphic. Place at bottom of project, stretch to fit, as shown in illustration. Press Tab and Done when finished placing element.

8. Select Fill In or Edit.

9. Edit row graphic: • Choose Baseball & Bat graphic. • Done.

10. To fill in a calendar day, edit the calendar block and choose Edit a Day from the menu list. Proceed to pick a day, and add text or graphic, or even a circled date.

Other Ideas Hang your calendar in a visible place, such as on a refrigerator door, for all to see. Print out extra graphics to cut and paste onto the calendar as needed.

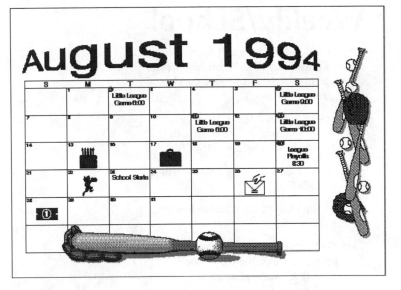

Here's a similar project idea for a monthly calendar for spring.

1. Select: • Calendar. • Design Your Own. • Calendar type. • Calendar year. • Calendar month.

2. Select Graphic: • Choose Full Panel. • Choose Irises.

3. Select Message: • Choose Lassen, Solid. • Type month and message, if you want.

4. Select Middle of Calendar: • Edit calendar to include your own text. • Add graphics as needed.

5. Select Graphic: • Choose Medium Staggered. • Choose Graphics, Daisies.

Weekly/School

Weekly calendars are great for tracking daily events. This PSD-Windows project shows a nifty weekly school calendar for the month of April.

1. Select: • **Calendar.** • **Weekly.** • **Tall.** • Choose a year, month, and specific week. • Click OK.

2. Select a Backdrop: • Choose Kites. • Click OK.

3. Select a Layout: • Choose Kites #2. • Click OK.

4. Edit text block (at bottom of project): • Double-click block. • **F**ont: Chaucer, Font **S**ize: Medium. • Click OK.

5. Fill in the individual day entries with text and graphics pertaining to your weekly schedule. To edit, double-click the calendar block. Pick a day and choose to add text or graphic, or a circled date. Click OK, and the text or graphic dialog boxes will appear, allowing you to type text or pick a graphic. Click OK when finished.

Other Ideas Print out and copy a month's worth of blank weekly calendars to distribute to everyone in the office. They can fill in their own schedules and appointments!

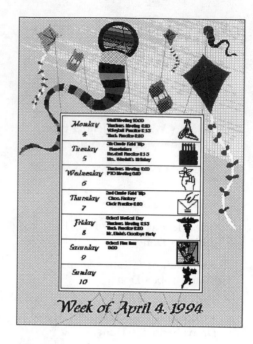

Week of April 4, 1994

You won't be able to create the project shown, but here's an attractive alternative for school.

1. Select: • Calendar. • Design Your Own. • Calendar type. • Calendar year. • Calendar month. • Calendar week.

2. Select Graphic: • Choose Full Panel. • Choose Books.

3. Select Message: • Choose Imperial, Solid. • Type message, if you want.

4. Select Middle of Calendar: • Edit calendar to include your own text. • Add graphics as needed.

5. Select Graphic: • Choose Small Staggered. • Choose Graphics, Books.

Daily/Business

A daily calendar can help you organize each hour of your day. Follow these PSD-DOS project steps for creating a daily calendar to use at work.

1. Select: • Calendar. • Create a New Project. • Tall. • Calendar type. • Calendar year. • Month. • Day. • Starting hour.

2. Select a **Backdrop:** • Choose Winter Snowscape. • **Done.**

3. Select a Layout: • Choose Winter Snowscape #1.

4. Select **F**ill In or Edit.

5. Edit headline block: • Tab. • Shape: Round Top. • Font: Subway. • Style: Double Blend effect with thick outline letters. • **Done.**

6. Fill in the individual hour entries with text and graphics pertaining to your daily schedule. Just edit the calendar block and choose **E**dit an Hour from the menu. Proceed to select hour, text, or graphic.

Other Ideas Design a month's worth of daily schedules, punch holes along the left edge, and bind them in a 3-ring notebook. This makes a great day planner for yourself, or to give to someone else!

Here's a variation for you to try:

1. Select: • Calendar. • Design Your Own. • Calendar type. • Calendar month. • Calendar year. • Calendar day.

2. Select Graphic: • Choose Full Panel. • Choose FromDesk.

3. Select Message: • Choose Madera, Solid. • Type message, if you want.

4. Select Middle of Calendar: • Edit calendar to include your own text. • Add graphics as needed.

Calendars

Event Calendar/ School

If your school, office, or family likes to organize schedules around events, design your own event calendar that clearly marks a month's worth of activities. Use event calendars to help keep school or office staff informed of important monthly happenings. The PSD-DOS project on this page shows how to make a seasonal event calendar for school.

1. Select: • Calendar. • Create a New Project. • Wide. • Calendar type. • Calendar year. • Month.

2. Select a **B**ackdrop: • Choose Bats & Pumpkins patterned backdrop. • **D**one.

3. Select a **L**ayout: • Choose Bats & Pumpkins 2.

4. Select **F**ill In or Edit.

5. Edit column graphic: • Tab. • **D**elete graphic block. • **D**one.

6. Edit calendar block: • **F**ont: New Zurica. • **D**one.

7. Edit headline block: • Tab. • **F**ont: Boulder. • **C**olors, Behind Text: Yellow. • **M**ove block up to make room for square graphic block below. • **D**one.

8. Select **A**dd New Elements, add: • **S**quare Graphic. • Add as many text blocks as needed to mark important weeks, as shown in project illustration. Press Tab and **D**one after placing each element.

9. Select **F**ill In or Edit.

10. Edit square graphic block: • Choose Pumpkin. • **F**rame: Drop Shadow. • **S**cale to fill space below headline block. • **D**one.

11. Edit text blocks: • Fill in and place your event text where needed on calendar.

Other Ideas   Clubs, community organizations, churches, and other groups will find this project idea useful in many ways. Event calendars make great mailers, too!

Team Calendar/ School

Keeping track of sports schedules can be a breeze with the Print Shop programs. Here's a project idea for keeping monthly team games organized at school.

1. Select: • Calendar. • New Project. • Tall. • Calendar type. • Calendar year. • Month.

2. Select Layout: • Choose layout 6.

3. Select Fill In or Edit.

4. Edit text block: • Stretch block across top of project. • Type team name on first line. • Boulder, 52-point size. • Drop shadow. • Type title of game schedule on second line. • Moderne, medium size • Colors, green behind text. • No frame.

5. Edit calendar block: • New Zurica.

6. Edit row graphic: • Choose Football Players. • Stretch to fill space at bottom of project.

7. Select Add New Elements, add: • Text block.

8. Select Fill In or Edit.

9. Edit text block: • Type information about the next month's schedule. • Scale to fit at bottom of calendar block, across empty day boxes.

10. Fill in your individual team schedules and add graphics.

Calendars

Wedding Planner/Home

Design a wedding planner for yourself or a friend to keep track of numerous wedding preparations. This is a wonderful idea for a bridal shower or engagement gift. Create as many months or weeks as needed, bind them, design an attractive cover, and you've made a clever planner to use for yourself or give to someone.

1. Select: • **Calendar.** • **Weekly.** • **Tall.** • Choose a year, month, and specific week. • Click OK.

2. Select a Backdrop: • Choose Lilies & Birds. • Click OK.

3. Select a Layout: • Choose Lilies & Birds 2. • Click OK.

4. Edit headline block: • Double-click block. • Font: Paramount, Style: Bold on. • Type WEDDING PLANNER on first line, all capital letters. Type the week on the second line, upper- and lowercase letters. • Click OK.

5. Edit calendar block: • Pull down the **P**roject menu. • Select **C**alendar Options. • **F**ont: New Zurica. • Click OK.

6. To edit individual daily entries, double-click the calendar block. Pick a day and choose to add text or graphic, or a circled date. Click OK, and the text or graphic dialog boxes will appear, allowing you to type text or pick a graphic. Click OK when finished. Try using Calligrapher font for this project.

Here's a variation of a wedding planner that you can try:

1. Select: • Calendar. • Design Your Own. • Calendar type. • Calendar month. • Calendar year. • Calendar week.

2. Select Graphic: • Choose Medium Ends. • Choose Graphics, Daisies.

3. Select Message: • Choose Lassen, Solid. • Type Wedding Planner on first line, upper- and lowercase letters. • Type month and week on second line, all uppercased letters. • Press F8 to Center.

4. Select Ruled Line: • Choose Double Line.

5. Select Middle of Calendar: • Edit calendar to include your own text. • Add graphics as needed.

6. Select Graphic: • Choose Small Staggered. • Choose Graphics, Daisies.

Design Tip

Modify the project above to become a shower planner for a baby or wedding shower. Use several weeks' worth of dates to help you organize party details.

Vacation Schedules/ Business

Here's a PSD-DOS project idea to help you keep track of everyone's vacation schedules at the office. This is also a good idea for school or home.

1. Select: • Calendar. • Create a New Project. • Tall. • Calendar type. • Calendar year.

2. Select a Backdrop: • Choose Coastal Scene. • Done.

3. Select a Layout: • Choose Coastal Scene 2.

4. Select Fill In or Edit.

5. Edit calendar block: • Font: Moderne. • Frame: Thick Line. • Done.

6. Edit headline block (year): • Tab. • Font: Tubular. • Done.

7. Edit bottom text block: • Tab. • Font: Heather, Font Size: 20-point. • Line Justify: Center, Placement: Center. • Tab. • Type EMPLOYEE VACATION SCHEDULES, two lines, all uppercase letters. • Tab. • Done.

8. Select Add New Elements, add: • Text Block. Place block in upper left corner of project. Press Tab and Done.

9. Select Fill In or Edit.

10. Edit new text block: • Tab. • Font: Steamer, Font Size: Small. • Line Justify: Center, Placement: Center. • Type your company department or heading. • Tab. • Done.

Calendar Tip Having trouble marking all the vacation schedules on an 8 1/2" x 11" sheet? Enlarge the calendar on a copying machine to make a big poster.

PSD Screened Background Tip To create a calendar project with a screened art block, follow this example:

1. After designing a calendar and editing the layout, choose a square graphic that you want to place in the background, such as World.

2. Scale the graphic and place on top of the calendar block, or wherever you want the art to appear.

3. Edit the color shading of the graphic to 30% or 40%.

4. Order the graphic to the back of the project (layer).

5. Edit calendar block, and make sure the color background is clear.

This should produce a calendar with a large picture shaded behind the months. Make sure you select bold, heavy lines and text for the calendar to show up on top of the shaded art.

Calendars

Advent Calendar/ Holiday

Advent calendars are special gifts for children counting down the days to Christmas. Each day of the calendar has a cut-out window, or flap to reveal a picture underneath. The picture can be a part of a larger drawing, or individual graphics beneath each flap. Each day of the month is revealed one at a time. Use your imagination to make a creative advent calendar for your family. These PSD-DOS project steps will start you off!

1. Select: • Calendar. • Create a New Project. • Tall. • Calendar type. • Calendar year. • Calendar month.

2. Select a Layout: • Choose Calendar 10.

3. Select Fill In or Edit.

4. Edit calendar block: • Font: New Zurica. • Frame: No Frame. • Done.

5. Edit headline block (month): • Tab. • Font: Calligrapher. • Done.

6. Select Add New Elements, add: • Row Graphic. Place block in bottom week of calendar across empty day boxes. Stretch to fit as shown in illustration. Press Tab and Done when finished.

7. Select Fill In or Edit.

8. Edit new graphic block: • Choose Nativity. • Done.

9. Using an X-acto knife or scissors, cut out the flaps, or windows, for each day box that will reveal a picture. Be careful not to cut out the entire day box, just portions of

the paper to be lifted up and peaked under.

10. Design and print out another calendar duplicating the one made in the steps above, except fill in the boxes for each day with a graphic. (You can also choose a large graphic and design your calendar to reveal a piece of the picture each day.)

11. Carefully, using glue, attach the graphic calendar to the back of the first calendar sheet created. Make sure the flaps you have cut will open to reveal a picture on the calendar underneath.

Another Idea Another option is to paste small graphics printed out from other project pages onto a blank sheet of paper. Attach this paper behind the calendar made in steps 1–8 above. Make sure the pictures line up under the flaps to be opened for each day. Or you might even try attaching holiday treats, sequins, glitter, and so on, under the flaps to be opened.

Parties, Holidays & Other Celebrations

Within this next group of projects, you'll find ideas for every kind of party or holiday get-together, including decorations, games, wrapping paper, and more. These ideas will use a variety of project types: greeting cards, signs, banners, and letterhead. If you're at all unclear about the menu sequences for a particular party project, refer to previous parts pages in Section 3 that show the menus for creating that project type.

When you're designing your own projects for celebrating, don't forget signs, banners, flags, wrappings, cards, placemats, and flyers for holidays and occasions like these:

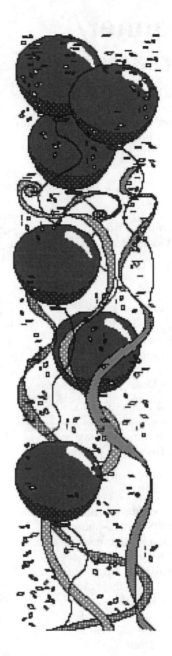

New Year's Eve	Grand opening parties
Valentine's Day	Open house parties
President's Day	Baby and bridal showers
Easter parade	Bon voyage parties
Fourth of July	Graduation parties
Halloween	School events
Thanksgiving	Company picnics
Hanukkah	Cookouts and barbecues
Christmas	Fall and spring festivals
Anniversary parties	Election parties

Party Banner/ Anniversary

Every party needs a banner. Anniversaries are no exception, whether it's a wedding anniversary or a company anniversary. Here's a simple wedding anniversary banner you can create using PSD-DOS.

1. Select: • Banner. • Create a New Project. • Horizontal.

2. Select a **B**ackdrop: • Choose Doves & Ribbons. • **D**one.

3. Select a **L**ayout: • Choose layout **3**.

4. Select **F**ill In or Edit.

5. Edit headline: • Tab. • Fo**n**t: Subway, Font **S**ize: Medium/ Medium. • **S**hape: Top Arch. • Tab. • Type "Happy Anniversary," two lines, all capital letters. • Tab. • **D**one.

6. Select **A**dd New Elements, add: • Text **B**lock. Place block below headline and fill remaining space. press Tab and **D**one after placing element.

7. Select **F**ill In or Edit.

8. Edit text block: • Tab. • Fo**n**t: Sherwood, Font **S**ize: 120-point. • Line **J**ustify: Center, **P**lacement: Center. • Tab. • Type "DAVE & PAT" (substitute your anniversary couple's names), two lines, capital letters. • Tab. • Fo**n**t: Boulder, Font **S**ize: X-small. • **C**olors, Text: Blue. • Tab. • Type "50 Years!," capital letters. • **D**one.

Other Ideas Try turning your banners into streamers. Choose a graphic or pattern to spread out all over your banner. Print it out, then cut the banner into two streamers. Tape the streamers to a doorway, ceiling, or even a fan! To put some bounce in your streamers, fold them accordion-style and hang.

You won't be able to duplicate the banner shown, but here's a nice alternative.

1. Select: • Banner. • Design Your Own. • Horizontal.

2. Select Graphic: • Choose Full Panel on Both Ends. • Choose Graphics, Party.

3. Select Message: • Choose Large Line Over Small. • Choose Madera, Solid. • Type "HAPPY ANNIVERSARY" on one line, and your wedding couple's names on the second line.

4. Select Trim: • Choose Thin, Deco.

Decorations/ Holiday

Add a festive touch to your home, office, or store window with decorative holiday signs and banners designed with the Print Shop programs. Follow these PSD-Windows steps to create a Christmas sign to place on a window or door.

1. Select: • **S**ign. • **T**all.

2. Select a Backdrop: • Blank Page. • Click OK.

3. Select a Layout: • No Layout. • Click OK.

4. With the New Object tool from the Tool palette, add: • **S**quare Graphic. • Two **H**eadline Blocks. Place one headline at the very top, one at the very bottom. Place the graphic in the center and size as shown in illustration.

5. Edit square graphic: • Double-click block. • Choose Candy Cane. • Click OK. • Scale graphic as large as possible.

6. Edit headline block 1: • Scale block to fill top width of sign. • Double-click block. • **F**ont: Chaucer, **J**ustify: Center. • **S**hape: Double Arch Up. • Type "Merry," upper- and lowercase letters. • Click OK.

7. Edit headline block 2: • Scale block to fill bottom width of sign. • Double-click block. • **F**ont: Chaucer, **J**ustify: Center. • **S**hape: Double Arch Up. • Type "Christmas," upper- and lowercase letters. • Click OK.

Here are steps for creating a similar Christmas sign on your program:

1. Select: • Sign or Poster. • Design Your Own. • Tall.

2. Select Border: • Wide, Holly.

3. Select Graphic: • Choose Medium Centered. • Choose Graphics, Poinsettia.

4. Select Message: • Choose Merced, Solid. • Type "Merry Christmas," upper- and lowercase letters, two lines with three empty lines in-between them. • Press F8 to center.

Design Tip

Use several sign designs to decorate a front door or window with holiday pictures and messages. This is a fun project for kids to do on a rainy day. Don't forget to add color and glue on glitter or sequins to make your holiday signs stand out.

Games/ Birthday Party

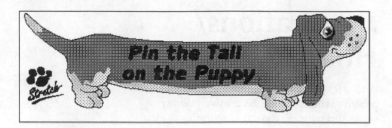

You can use the Print Shop programs to make all sorts of party games for children and adults. Here's a PSD-DOS project idea for a variation of the ever-popular birthday game, Pin-the-Tail-on-the-Donkey.

1. Select: • Banner. • Create a New Project. • Horizontal.

2. Select a **B**ackdrop: • Choose Stretch Dog. • **D**one.

3. Select a **L**ayout: • Choose layout 1.

4. Select **F**ill In or Edit.

5. Edit headline block: • **F**ont: Tubular. • **Sh**ape: Rectangle. • Tab. • Type "Pin the Tail on the Puppy," upper- and lowercase letters. • Tab. • Done.

You can create a sign project that can be printed out in a large size to make a poster variation of this project idea. Substitute a teddy bear for the puppy shown above.

1. Select: • Sign or Poster. • Design Your Own. • Tall.

2. Select Graphic: • Choose Large Centered. • Choose Graphics, Teddy Bear.

3. Select Message: • Choose Amador, Solid. • Type "Pin the Bow on the Bear," upper- and lowercase letters, two lines with three empty lines in-between them. • Press F8 to center.

4. Print out bear and color it in. Use construction paper to make bows to be pinned on by the game participants.

Design Tip

After printing out the banner, cut out the dog's shape, minus the tail. Attach to a wall or outdoor fence. Make separate tails out of construction paper for children to pin.

Gift Tags/ Christmas

The greeting-card type of project also makes great gift tags for any occasion. To make a miniature card as a gift tag, just print out your project at 50 percent of its original size. Follow the PSD-DOS steps below to make a Christmas gift tag.

1. Select: • Greeting Card. • Create a New Project. • Side Fold.

2. Select **A**dd New Elements, add. • **S**quare Graphic. Place graphic in middle of card and size as large as possible. Press Tab and **D**one when finished placing element.

3. Select **F**ill In or Edit.

4. Edit square graphic: • Choose Holly. • **D**one.

5. Select **I**nside of Card.

6. Select **A**dd New Elements, add: • **S**quare Graphic. • **H**eadline Block. Place graphic in upper half of space, size to fill space. Place headline block in lower half of space and size to fit. Press Tab and **D**one after placing each element.

7. Select **F**ill In or Edit.

8. Edit graphic block: • Choose Holly. • **D**one.

9. Edit headline block: • Tab. • **F**ont: Signature, **J**ustify: Center. • **S**hape: Slant Left. • Tab. • Press the Spacebar twice; type "Merry Christmas," two lines, upper- and lowercase letters. • Tab. • **D**one.

10. When you're ready to print, select **P**rint and choose Output Size from the Print Options menu. Change output to 50%. Print your card, fold it and you're done!

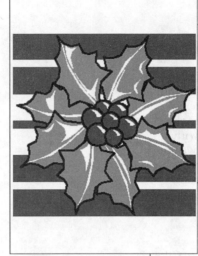

Other Ideas   Make wrapping paper that matches your gift tag design by following the steps on the next page.

Design Tip
For a really tiny gift tag, print your card at 25% of its original size.

Parties, Holidays & Other Celebrations

Wrapping Paper/Birthday

Believe it or not, you can even make your own wrapping paper using your computer! Simply design a pattern using various backdrops and graphic blocks. Print it out and color it with markers or paint. What a great way to create personalized wrapping paper for any occasion. The steps below show how to make wrapping paper using PSD-Windows.

1. Select: • **S**ign. • **T**all.

2. Select a Backdrop: • Choose Gifts pattern. • Click OK.

3. Select a Layout: • Choose No Layout. • Click OK.

4. Use the New Object tool to add: • Eight **S**quare Graphics. • Stagger each block across the page as shown in illustration.

5. Edit square graphics: • Double-click a square graphic block. • Choose Birthday Hippo. • Choose Apply to All Squares. • Click OK.

Other Ideas   Make a gift tag that matches your wrapping paper design by following the project steps on the previous page.

Here's a similar wrapping paper design you can make using NPS.

1. Select: • Sign or Poster. • Design Your Own. • Tall.

2. Select Graphic: • Choose Small Staggered. • Choose Graphics, Balloons.

3. Print your sign, color it in, and you're ready to wrap!

Design Tip

If one printed page isn't enough to wrap your gift, print out several copies and tape them together to form a larger sheet of wrap.

Games/Baby Shower

Use the notepad orientation from the letterhead project type to make game forms for baby or bridal showers. The form will print two to a page. Have the form copied on a copier. You're all set with a party game to hand out to each guest. Follow these PSD-DOS steps to create a shower game.

1. Select: • Letterhead. • Create a New Project. • Notepad.

2. Select a **Backdrop**: • Choose Wet Duck. • **Done**.

3. Select **Add New Elements**, add • Border. • Headline Block. • Three **Text** Blocks. Place headline at top of project, and one text block below the headline. Place the other two text blocks side by side, like columns (see illustration). Size each block to use maximum space. Press Tab and **Done** after placing each element.

4. Select **F**ill In or Edit.

5. Edit border: • Choose Thin Border. • **Done**.

6. Edit headline block: • Tab. • F**ont**: Scribble, Line Justify: Center. • **Shape**: Arc Up. • Tab. • Type "WELCOME TO MELISSA'S BABY SHOWER" (substitute your guest of honor's name), upper- and lowercase letters. • Tab. • **Done**.

7. Edit text block 1: • Tab. • **Font**: New Zurica, Font **Size**: 14-point. • Line Justify: Center, Placement: Center.• Tab. • Type "You're now an official contestant in our Perilous Purse Scavenger Hunt. Look through your purse for any of the items listed below. Tally up your points and wait to see if you won! Good luck!," five lines, upper- and lowercase letters. • Tab. • **Done**.

8. Edit text block 2: • Tab. • Font: Jester, Font Size: 14-point. • Line Justify: Left, Placement: Top. • Tab. • Type a list of items that may be found in a purse. • Tab. • Done.

9. Edit text block 3: • Tab. • Font: Jester, Font **Size**: 14-point. • Line Justify: Left, Placement: Top. • Tab. • Type a list of items that may be found in a purse. • Tab. • Done.

Design Tip

When placing text blocks over graphics or backdrop art, be sure to choose a bold font with a large enough point size to be legible. The design of the art behind the text often makes it hard to read type layered on top so use caution.

Placecards/
Holiday

You can design instant placecards for holiday dinners, or other seated occasions. Create your card using the greeting-card project type. Print out your project at 50 percent of its original size. The PSD-Windows steps below show how to make a Thanksgiving dinner placecard.

1. Select: • **G**reeting Card. • **T**op Fold.

2. Select a Backdrop: • Choose Blank Page. • Click OK.

3. Select a Layout: • Choose No Layout. • Click OK.

4. With the New Object tool, add: • **S**quare Graphic. • **H**orizontal Ruled Line. • **T**ext Block. Place the graphic block in the left half of the card, and the text block in the right half. Place the ruled line above and size across top.

5. Edit square graphic: • Scale to fill space as shown in illustration. • Double-click block. • Choose Apple Basket. • Click OK.

6. Edit text block: • Scale to fill space as shown in illustration. • Double-click block. • **F**ont: Calligrapher, Size: Large, Justification: **H**orizontal Center. • Type family member's name, two lines, upper- and lowercase letters. • Click OK.

7. Edit ruled line: • Double-click block. • Choose Flower & Vines. • Click OK.

Other Ideas   Be creative and add decorations to your placecards; glue on silk flowers, lace, candy corn, ribbons, dried flowers, candy canes, and more.

Here's a decorative placecard design you can make using NPS.

1. Select: • Greeting Card. • Design Your Own. • Top Fold.

2. Select Border: • Choose Wide, Columns.

3. Select Message: • Choose Lassen, Solid. • Type in the name of your guest on two lines, upper- and lowercase letters. • Press F8 to center.

Design Tip

Placecards work best as top-fold greeting-card projects. You can personalize each placecard on your computer before you print them out.

Party Favors/ Holiday

Use the Print Shop programs to design simple party favors for any party; paper baskets, folded paper boxes, teepees, or origami sculptures.

Here's an easy idea for Halloween party favors. Use the sign project to create a festive pattern. Print it out on relatively thin (or lightweight) paper. Add color to the printout with markers or paint. Place your paper on a table, design side down. Take a handful of candies and place in the center of the paper. Now pull up all four corners and edges of the paper and wrap the candies inside the page, rather like a pouch. Tie the favor shut with colorful curling ribbon. You've got an instant party favor! Follow these PSD-DOS steps to make your design:

1. Select: • Sign. • Create a New Project. • Wide.

2. Select a Backdrop: • Choose Bats & Pumpkins. • Done.

Other Ideas   Any craft projects that are made out of paper can be made with your Print Shop printouts. To see what other crafty paper projects you can create, explore craft books at your local library or bookstore.

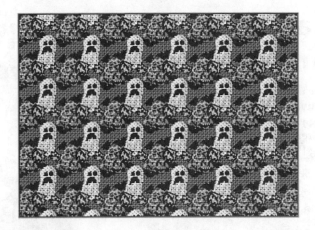

You can make a similar design by using a sign project and selecting a small, staggered graphic layout.

Here's an idea to try:

1. Select: • Sign or Poster. • Design your Own. • Wide.

2. Select Graphic: • Choose Small Staggered. • Choose a festive graphic such as Balloons, Party Favor, or Ice Cream.

Placemats/ Birthday

You can easily design party placemats for any holiday or special gathering using your computer. Here's a simple children's birthday party placemat idea using PSD-Windows.

1. Select: • **Sign**. • **Wide**.

2. Select a Backdrop: • Choose Dino Birthday. • Click OK.

3. Select a Layout: • Choose No Layout. • Click OK.

4. Use the New Object tool to add: • **Headline Block**. Place block across top of project, as shown in illustration.

5. Edit headline block: • Double-click block. • Font: New Zurica, Style: Bold on, Justify: Center. • Shape: Top Arch. • Type "Matt is 6 years old!" (substitute your child's name and age), two lines, upper- and lowercase letters. • Click OK.

Other Ideas Set out crayons as party favors and let kids color in their placemats. Have a contest and give a prize for the best-looking placemat. If you're using PSD (DOS or Windows), you can even print out the placemats using the Coloring Book option!

You can make similar placemats using your program version. Here's how:

1. Select: • Sign or Poster. • Design Your Own. • Wide.

2. Select Graphic: • Choose Small Rows. • Choose a different graphic for each block, such as sports pictures.

3. Select Message: • Choose Marin, Solid. • Type in the name of your birthday guest and a birthday phrase. • Press F8 to center.

Reunion Banner/Home

Big parties call for big signs. Use the Print Shop programs to make creative banners for your large gatherings. The following PSD-Windows steps show how to make a directional banner for a family reunion.

1. Select: • **B**anner. • **H**orizontal.

2. Select a Backdrop: • Choose Balloons. • Click OK.

3. Select a Layout: • Choose Balloons 2. • Click OK.

4. Edit headline block: • Double-click block. • **F**ont: Bazooka, Si**z**e: Large Over Small. • **S**hape: Rectangle. • Type "SMITH REUNION UP AHEAD" (substitute your family name), two lines, all capital letters. • Click OK.

Other Ideas   Make banners for all your reunion activities, pie-eating contests, sack-race finish lines, even pennants for the big softball game!

Here's a reunion banner that's simple to make:

1. Select: • Banner. • Design Your Own. • Horizontal.

2. Select Graphic: • Choose Large Graphic Both Ends. • Choose Graphics, Picnic.

3. Select Message: • Choose Two Equal Lines. • Sutter, Solid. • Type in your reunion message. • Press F8 to center.

Design Tip

Don't get overzealous with your banner creations and try to fit too much text onto a banner. The rule "less is more" applies here. Also, if your banner is to be read at quite some distance, use a bold, blocky font in a really large point size.

Other Business Projects

This next group of projects features ideas for your business, whether it's an office, restaurant, or store. You'll find ideas for every kind of professional use, including newsletters, forms, cover sheets, and more. These ideas will use a variety of project types: letterhead, signs, greeting cards, and others. If you're at all unclear about the menu sequences for a particular business project, refer to previous parts pages in Section 3 that show the menus for creating that project type.

As you're thinking about different business project ideas you can use around your office, store, or staff—try these:

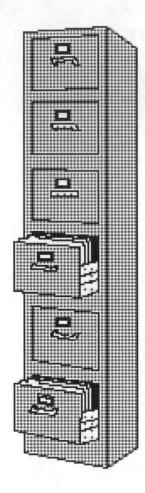

Mailing labels

Charts

Equipment labels

Invoices

Coupons

Order forms

Phone number lists

Interoffice documents

To Do lists

Sign-up sheets

Filing labels

Package labels

Fax cover sheets

Nametags

Bulletin board notices

Presentation programs

Menus

Brochures

Presentation banners

Daily report sheets

Employee-of-the-Month awards

Address lists

Report cover sheets

Rolodex cards

Inspirational messages

Handouts

Accounting sheets

Time sheets

Office door signs

File cabinet labels

Receipts

Office calendar

Employee vacation calendar

Business cards

Newsletter

Newsletters can help you get the word out about office promotions and policies, upcoming sale events, volunteer activities, and more. The project idea on this page shows you how to create a simple, one-page newsletter promoting local events related to your business. This PSD-DOS project is a great idea for mailing or handing out to customers.

1. Select: • Letterhead. • Create a New Project. • Regular.

2. Select Add New Elements; add • Headline Block. • Two Square Graphics. • Three Text Blocks. Place headline block at very top and size to fill width, as shown in illustration. Place one square graphic beneath headline, left side. Place the other square graphic in bottom right corner. Place one text block beneath headline, beside first square graphic. Place other two text blocks side by side, as columns (see illustration). Press Tab and Done after placing each element.

3. Select Fill In or Edit.

4. Edit headline (top): • Tab. • Font: Heather. • Shape: Arc Up. • Tab. • Type "The Music News" (substitute your newsletter name), upper- and lowercase letters. • Tab. • Done.

5. Edit square graphic 1 (top left): • Choose Music, or a graphic pertaining to your company. • Enlarge slightly to fill space if needed, as shown in illustration. • Done.

6. Edit text block 1 (beneath headline): • Tab. • Font: NewZuricaBold. • Line Justify: Center, Placement: Center. • Frame: Drop Shadow. • Tab. • Type your company name, address and phone number, as many lines as needed. • Tab. • Done.

7. Edit text block 2 (left column): • Tab. • Font: Paramount, Font Size: 14-point. • Line Justify: Left, Placement: Top. • Frame: Thin Line. • Tab. • Type your newsletter article. • Tab. • Done.

8. Edit text block 3 (right column): • Tab. • Font: Paramount, Font Size: 14-point. • Line Justify: Left, Placement: Top. • Tab. • Type another newsletter article. • Tab. • Done.

9. Edit square graphic 2 (bottom right): • Choose A to Z, or a graphic pertaining to your article. You may have to resize graphic to fit space. • Done.

Other Ideas If your newsletter needs more pages, just create a new sign project for each page needed. You can run them through a copier to print both sides of the newsletter paper. To use your newsletter as a mailer, create a design for the back of the newsletter that has three horizontal panels (trifold). The top two horizontal panels can have more newsletter articles and art. The bottom panel can be designed with room for a mailing label and a stamp.

Design Tips

Be careful not to clutter your newsletter with too many blocks of text and art. The two-text column approach will provide you with the greatest readability. It's a good idea to find copies of other newsletters you like. They will give you good ideas to follow with your own newsletter projects.

Order Forms

You can make simple order forms using PSD. The notepad orientation of the letterhead project type makes them easy to create. Plus, you'll be able to print two to a page. Follow these PSD-Windows steps to make a general company order form:

1. Select: • **L**etterhead. • **S**ingle Page.

2. Select a Backdrop: • Choose Blank Page. • Click OK.

3. Select a Layout: • Choose No Layout. • Click OK.

4. With the New Object tool, add: • **R**ow Graphic. • **H**eadline. • **T**wo Text Blocks. Place the row graphic at top and stretch across width. Place the headline on top of row graphic. Place one text block below row graphic, and the second text block below the first. Size blocks as shown in example.

5. Edit row graphic: • Double-click block. • Choose Orange Slices. • Click OK.

6. Edit headline: • Stretch to fill space between oranges in row graphic. • Double-click block. • **F**ont: New Zurica. • **S**hape: Top Arch. • Type your company name, two lines, all capital letters. • Click OK.

7. Edit text block 1 (beneath row graphic): • Double-click block. • **F**ont: New Zurica, Size: Medium, Justification: **H**orizontal Center. • Type title of order form, all capital letters. • Click OK. • Choose the Frame tool and select a Thin Line frame. • Choose background color Blue from the color palette.

8. Edit text block 2: • Double-click on block. • **F**ont: New Zurica, Size: Small, Justification: **H**orizontal Left. • Type your order form information, use the Spacebar to space out words, if needed. Use the Shift key and the hyphen key (-) to make lines. • Click OK. • With the Frame Tool, select a Thin Line frame for the block.

Other Ideas   Use your Print Shop program to design all sorts of office documentation. Adding crisp graphics can call attention to any form you use in your office or store.

Labels

Design your own labels for mailing packages, file folders, equipment, and more. Here's a project idea for a mailing label created with the notepad orientation of the letterhead project type. Follow the PSD-DOS steps below:

1. Select: • Letterhead. • Create a New Project. • Notepad.

2. Select **A**dd New Elements; add • **T**ext Block. • **S**quare Graphic. Use just the top half of the Notepad project space. Place the text block at the very top. Place the square graphic in the lower right corner, as shown in illustration. Press Tab and **D**one after placing each element.

3. Select **F**ill In or Edit.

4. Edit text block: • Tab. • Fo**n**t: Jester, Font **S**ize: Medium. • Line **J**ustify: Left, Placement: Top. • **F**rame: Thick Line. • Tab. • Type your company name and address, upper- and lowercase letters. • Tab. • **D**one.

5. Edit square graphic: • Choose Apple Basket, or a graphic pertaining to your company. • Move block to fit inside lower right corner of text block. • Enlarge slightly, as shown in illustration. • **D**one.

You can create labels using the greeting-card project type. Follow these steps to create a mailing label:

1. Select: • Greeting Card. • Design Your Own. • Top Fold.

2. Select Border: • Choose Thin, Ribbon.

3. Select Graphic: • Choose Small Centered. • Choose an appropriate graphic to go with your company, such as Computer.

4. Select Customize: • Move the small graphic to the upper left corner of the project.

5. Select Message: • Choose Small, Solid. • Starting with a line below the graphic block, type your company name and address on three lines. • Align each line to the left, using the F6 key.

6. If you need to create two labels to a page, repeat these steps on the inside of the card.

Menus

You can quickly design all kinds of menus for your restaurant, company dinner, or other special events requiring a menu. There are numerous food-related graphics you can choose. This project idea shows how to make a very simple menu using PSD-Windows.

1. Select: • **Sign.** • **Tall.**

2. Select a Backdrop: • Choose Blank Page. • Click OK.

3. Select a Layout: • Choose No Layout. • Click OK.

4. With the New Object tool, add • **Column Graphic.** • **Headline.** • **Text Block.** Position graphic block at left side of space, size to fit from top to bottom. Place headline at top right side of project, size as shown illustration. Place text block below headline and fill remaining space.

5. Edit column graphic: • Double-click block. • Choose Mod Cafe Cups. • Click OK. • Use the Frame tool to choose a Drop Shadow frame. • Choose the color palette and select 80% shaded Blue background for graphic block.

6. Edit headline block: • Double-click block. • **F**ont: Sherwood. • **S**hape: Rectangle. • **J**ustify: Center. • Type "THE COFFEE HUT", capital letters, two lines as shown. • Click OK. • Use the Frame tool to choose a Drop Shadow frame. • Choose the color palette and select 80% shaded Yellow background.

7. Edit text block: • Double-click block. • **F**ont: Chaucer, Size: Medium, Justification: Horizontal Center. • Type in menu selections and prices. • Click OK.

Other Ideas   Laminate your menus to use them over and over! Also use the sign projects to post daily specials, or insert "Daily Special" flyers within your existing menus.

Coupons

Make your own coupons to distribute to your customers. Use the notepad orientation from the letterhead project type to design coupons for your products or services. Follow the PSD-DOS steps below:

1. Select: • Letterhead. • Create a New Project. • Notepad.

2. Select **A**dd New Elements; add • **Mini-Border, Small.** • **H**eadline. • **Text Block.** • **S**quare Graphic. Use just the top half of the Notepad project space. Place the mini-border as illustrated. Inside the mini-border, place the headline to stretch across space. Place the text block below the headline, on left side of coupon. Place the square graphic on the lower right side of coupon, opposite the text block. You may have to adjust your block sizes to fit properly. Press Tab or **D**one after placing each element.

3. Select **F**ill In or Edit.

4. Edit mini-border: • Choose Joined Lines, Large. • **D**one.

5. Edit headline block: • Tab. • Font: Boulder, Line Justify: Center. • **S**hape: Double Arch Up. • Tab. • Type "40% OFF!", or your coupon headline. • Tab. • **D**one.

6. Edit text block: • Tab. • Font: Use New Zurica for message, Subway for company name. • Font **S**ize: Use a smaller size for message and a large size for company name. • Line Justify: Center, Placement: Center. • Tab. • Type your coupon message, including company name and coupon expiration date. • Tab. • **D**one.

7. Edit square graphic: • Choose Pets, or a graphic pertaining to your company. • **D**one.

Other Ideas Use your coupons with mailings, advertising flyers, or newsletters. They're a great way to advertise and bring in business. Don't forget to include an expiration date!

Bulletin Board Notices

Use the sign project type to make all kinds of bulletin board notices, or other signs to post, including memos. Here's a quick project idea for soliciting participants for a corporate softball team. Follow these PSD-Windows steps:

1. Select: • **S**ign. • **T**all.

2. Select a Backdrop: • Choose Blank Page. • Click OK.

3. Select a Layout: • Choose Sign 2. • Click OK.

4. Edit square graphics: • Double-click first square graphic. • Choose Baseball. • Apply to All Squares, make all four graphic blocks the same. • Click OK.

5. Edit headline block: • Double-click block. • **F**ont: Boulder. • **S**hape: Rectangular. • Type "PLAY BALL!", capital letters. • Click OK.

6. Edit text block: • Double-click block. • **F**ont: Tribune. • **S**ize: Use different sizes for different parts of your message. • Justification: **H**orizontal Center. • Type in message details. • Click OK. • Use the Frame tool to select a Double Line frame.

Other Ideas Bulletin board notices can be used to promote company events, advertise open positions, recognize someone's hard work, provide sign-up sheets for special activities, solicit volunteer work, and more.

Here's a similar bulletin board notice you can make.

1. Select: • Sign or Poster. • Design Your Own. • Tall.

2. Select Border: • Choose Wide, Clipboard.

3. Select Graphic: • Choose Medium Centered. • Choose Graphics, Baseball.

4. Select Customize: • Move the graphic to the top of the project.

5. Select Message: • Choose Small, Solid. • Starting with a line below the graphic block, type your message. • Press F8 to center.

Inspirational Messages

Use Print Shop signs and banners to make inspirational messages for your staff, sales team, customer service center, and more. Here's an easy sign idea to make using PSD-DOS:

1. Select: • Sign. • Create a New Project. • Wide.

2. Select a Layout: • Choose Sign 17.

3. Select Fill In or Edit.

4. Edit border: • Choose Paper Clips, Large. • Done.

5. Edit headline block: • Tab. • Font: Subway. • Shape: Rectangular. • Tab. • Type "TEAMWORK", all capital letters. • Tab. • Done.

6. Edit text block: • Tab. • Font: Boulder, Font Size: Medium. • Line Justify: Center, Placement: Center. • Tab. • Type "YOU'RE THE PAPER CLIP THAT KEEPS US TOGETHER!," all capital letters, three lines as shown in illustration. • Tab. • Done.

Other Ideas   Use sign and banner projects to post sales goals, company mottos, motivational sayings, and other communication you want your staff or office to remember.

Follow these steps to create a similar inspirational message project.

1. Select: • Sign or Poster. • Design Your Own. • Wide.

2. Select Border: • Choose Wide. Clipboard.

3. Select Message: • Choose Madera, Solid. • Type an inspirational message appropriate to your office.

Other Business Projects

Fax Cover Sheets

When your company or office needs to send a fax, use a handy fax cover sheet made with the Print Shop programs. The project idea below shows how to make an eye-catching fax sheet using PSD-Windows.

1. Select: • **Sign.** • **Tall.**

2. Select a Backdrop: • Choose Blank Page. • Click OK.

3. Select a Layout: • Choose Sign 4. • Click OK.

4. Edit headline block: • Double-click block. • **Font:** Subway. • Type "FAX", capital letters. • Click OK.

5. Edit text block: • Double-click block. • **Font:** Subway, **Size:** 68-point, **Justification:** **H**orizontal Center, **V**ertical Full. • Type "TO: FROM: DATE: of PGS", and use the Shift key and the hyphen key to make lines as shown in illustration. • Click OK. • Use the Frame tool to select a Thick Line frame.

Other Ideas Once you've found a fax cover design you like, have it printed in large quantities to keep near your fax machine.

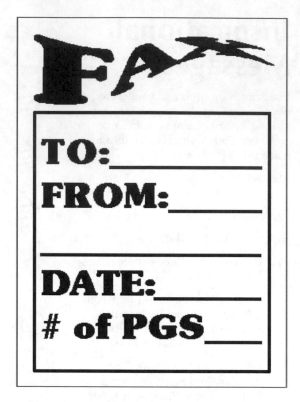

Here's a very simple fax cover sheet you can create using NPS.

1. Select: • Sign or Poster. • Design Your Own. • Tall.

2. Select Border: • Choose Thin, Ribbon.

3. Select Message: • Choose Amador, Solid. • Type same text as shown in the illustration. Hold down the Shift key and the hyphen key (-) to make lines. You might want to make the word "Fax" a larger point size than the rest of the text. • Press F8 to center.

Employee of the Month Award

Here's a great idea for recognizing your employees. Design an Employee of the Month award using PSD. Follow these simple PSD-DOS steps:

1. Select: • Sign. • Create a New Project. • Wide.

2. Select **Add** New Elements; add • **S**quare Graphic. • **H**eadline. • **T**ext Block. Enlarge the square graphic to fill entire space. Place the Headline inside square graphic and stretch across top, as shown in illustration. Place the text block below the headline and fill remaining space. Press Tab and **D**one after placing each element.

3. Select **F**ill In or Edit.

4. Edit square graphic: • Choose Other Libraries. • Choose Initial Caps, Stamp. • **D**one.

5. Edit headline block: • Tab. • Font: Sherwood • Shape: Arc Up. • Tab. • Type "EMPLOYEE OF THE MONTH", all capital letters, two lines. • Tab. • **D**one.

6. Edit text block: • Tab. • Font: Boulder, Font Size: 60-point. • Line Justify: Center, Placement: Center. • Colors, Behind Text: White. • Tab. • Type your employee's name. • Tab. • Font Size: Medium. • Tab. • Type accomplishment, and date. • Tab. • **D**one.

Other Ideas   Have your finished award copied onto parchment or other quality paper. You can then have it framed to hang in an office.

Follow these project steps to create a different Award.

1. Select: • Sign or Poster. • Design Your Own. • Tall.

2. Select Graphic: • Full Panel • Certificate.

3. Select Message: • Contrast the fancy type in the word "Certificate" with a font like Madera, or use a small script font, such as Merced. • Type your award message and press F10 to preview.

Report Cover Sheets

Putting together an important presentation? Make an effective title cover that's sure to stand out. Follow these PSD-Windows steps to make a report cover sheet.

1. Select: • **Sign.** • **Tall.**

2. Select a Backdrop: • Choose Blank Page. • Click OK.

3. Select a Layout: • Choose No Layout. • Click OK.

4. Use the New Object tool to add: • **M**ini-Border. • **T**ext Block. • **S**quare Graphic. Place the text block in the middle of the page, size as shown. Place the square graphic over the text block, size as shown. Place the mini-border around both text and graphic blocks.

5. Edit text block: • Double-click block. • **F**ont: Paramount, Style: Bold on, Justification: **H**orizontal Center. • Type report title. • Click OK.

6. Edit square graphic: • Double-click block. • Choose PSDeluxe Calendar Icons. • Choose Money. • Click OK. • Choose the color palette and shade the graphic 40%.

7. Edit mini-border: • Double-click block. • Choose Diamond Corners. • Click OK.

Other Ideas   You'll find dozens of uses for report cover sheets designed with your Print Shop program; employee manuals, training materials, client presentations, quotes, equipment operation instructions, and more.

Here's a very simple report cover sheet you can make using NPS.

1. Select: • Sign or Poster. • Design Your Own. • Tall.

2. Select Graphic: • Choose Small Centered. • Pick a graphic appropriate to your report subject.

3. Select Message: • Choose Small, Solid. • Type your report title, one line above graphic, one line below graphic. • Press F8 to center. If graphic is not quite aligned, select Customize and align the graphic horizontally or vertically.

Other School Projects

You'll find hundreds of things to make for your school or classroom with the Print Shop Programs. This next group of projects features ideas like school newsletters, award certificates, flashcards, and more. These ideas will use a variety of project types: letterhead, signs, greeting cards, and others. If you're at all unclear about the menu sequences for a particular school project, refer to previous parts pages in Section 3 that show the menus for creating that project type.

To get you started thinking about things you can make with your Print Shop programs, here's a list to spark your imagination:

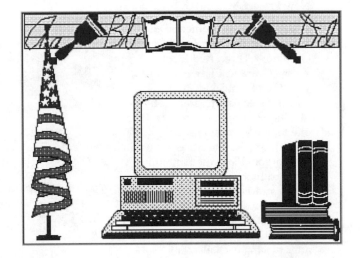

Class worksheets	Homework assignment sheets	Visuals
Language lab signs	Programs for school plays	Coloring pages
Class projects	Games	Book marks
Bulletin board notices	Club announcements	Programs for plays or assemblies
Cue cards for rehearsals	Science fair banners	Progress report sheets
Spelling bee banners	Sports banners	Pep rallies
Multiplication flashcards	Alphabet flashcards	Event calendars
Addition/subtraction flashcardz	Spelling flashcards	Choir and band concert signs

Newsletter

Newsletters can help you get the word out about school events and happenings. The project idea on this page shows you how to create a simple, one-page newsletter. This PSD-DOS project is a great idea for mailing or take-home handouts.

1. Select: • Letterhead. • Create a New Project. • Regular.

2. Select Add New Elements; add: • Headline Block. • Square Graphic. • Three Text Blocks. • Row Graphic. Place headline at very top of page and stretch across width. Place square graphic below headline in upper left corner. Place one text block beside square graphic and size to fit, as shown in illustration. Place the remaining two text blocks side by side, below in the middle of the page, as illustration shows. Place row graphic at very bottom, stretch across width. Press Tab and **Done** after placing each element.

3. Select **F**ill In or Edit.

4. Edit headline: • Tab. • Font: Heather. • **S**hape: Arc Up. • Tab. • Type "Wilson Elementary NEWS" (substitute your school name). • Tab. • **D**one.

5. Edit square graphic: • Choose A to Z, or a graphic pertaining to your school. • **D**one.

6. Edit text block 1 (below headline): • Tab. • Font: New Zurica. • Frame: Thin Line. • Tab. • Type your edition information, such as who worked on the newsletter, what month or week it's for, etc. You'll want to use different sizes for different parts of this text block. • Tab. • **D**one.

7. Edit text block 2 (left column): • Tab. • Font: Paramount, Font

Size: 14-point. • Line Justify: Left, Placement: Top. • Frame: Thin Line. • Tab. • Type your newsletter article. • Tab. • Done.

8. Edit text block 3 (right column): • Tab. • Font: Paramount, Font Size: 14-point. • Line Justify: Left, Placement: Top. • Tab. • Type another newsletter article. • Tab. • Done.

9. Edit row graphic: • Choose Parade, or a graphic pertaining to your article. • Done.

Other Ideas If your newsletter needs more pages, just create a new sign project for each page needed. You can run them through a copier to print both sides of the newsletter paper. To use your newsletter as a mailer, create a design for the back of the newsletter that has three horizontal panels (trifold). The top two horizontal panels can have more newsletter articles and art. The bottom panel can be designed with room for a mailing label and a stamp.

Design Tips

Be careful not to clutter your newsletter with too many blocks of text and art. The two-columns-of-text approach will provide you with the greatest readability. It's a good idea to find copies of other newsletters you like. They will give you good ideas to follow with your own newsletter projects.

Award Certificates

Certificates are a great idea for recognizing students, staff, or faculty. Design your own using your Print Shop program. Follow these simple PSD-Windows steps:

1. Select: • **Sign**. • **Wide**.

2. Select a Backdrop: • Choose Blank Page. • Click OK.

3. Select a Layout: • Choose No Layout. • Click OK.

4. With the New Object tool to add: • **Square Graphic**. • **Headline**. • **Text Block**. Size square graphic to fill entire space. Place headline inside square graphic and stretch across top. Place text block below headline and fill remaining space, as shown in illustration.

5. Edit square graphic: • Double-click block. • Choose PSDeluxe Initial Caps, choose Border & Stars. • Click OK.

6. Edit headline: • Double-click block. • **Font**: Sherwood. • **Shape**: Top Arch. • Type "MATH AWARD", all capital letters. • Click OK. • Make sure background color is Clear on the Color palette.

7. Edit text block: • Double-click block. • **Font**: Calligrapher, Size: Medium, Justification: **H**orizontal Center.• Type "For Outstanding Achievement in Mathematics, we hereby award highest honors to" and type in name of recipient, upper- and lowercase letters. • Click OK. • Choose the Color palette and select a White background behind text.

Other Ideas   Have your finished award copied onto parchment or other quality paper. You can then have it framed to hang.

Here are steps to create a certificate using NPS:

1. Select: • Sign or Poster. • Design Your Own. • Wide.

2. Select Graphic: • Choose Full Panel. • Choose Graphics, Medals.

3. Select Message: • Choose Tiny, Solid. • Start your first line below the graphic; type "For Outstanding Achievement in Mathematics, we hereby award highest honors to" and type in the name of the recipient, upper- and lowercase letters. • F10 to preview.

Other School Projects

Bulletin Board Notices

You can make all kinds of clever bulletin board notices to hang around the school or classroom. Here's a PSD-DOS idea for a club notice.

1. Select: • Sign. • Create a New Project. • Tall.

2. Select a-**B**ackdrop: • Choose UFO. • **D**one.

3. Select a-**L**ayout: • Choose UFO 1.

4. Select **F**ill In or Edit.

5. Edit headline 1 (upper left corner): • Font: Boulder. • Tab. • Type "HEY," all capital letters. • Tab. • **D**one.

6. Edit headline 2 (inside UFO): • Font: Stylus. • Tab. • Type "SCIENCE CLUB", all capital letters. • Tab. • **D**one.

7. Edit headline 3 (left beam): • **F**ont: Tubular. • Tab. • Type "MEET-ING", capital letters. • Tab. • **D**one.

8. Edit headline 4 (middle beam): • Font: Tubular. • Tab. • Type date of meeting. • Tab. • **D**one.

9. Edit headline 5 (right beam): • Font: Tubular. • Tab. • Type time of meeting. • Tab. • **D**one.

Here's a club notice for a choir group:

1. Select: • Sign or Poster. • Design Your Own. • Tall.

2. Select Graphic: • Choose Full Panel. • Choose Graphics, Juke-box.

3. Select Message: • Choose Small, Solid. • Starting with a line below the artwork, type a message such as "Jazz Choir Meeting Thursday, Sept. 8, 3:00 in the choir room. We'll be planning our fall musical presentation, costumes and choreography!" • Press F10 to preview.

Flashcards

You can design word flashcards, alphabet flashcards, addition and subtraction flashcards, and even multiplication cards. Follow these PSD-Windows steps to create the flashcards shown:

1. Select: • **Sign.** • **Tall.**

2. Select a Backdrop: • Choose Blank Page. • Click OK.

3. Select a Layout: • Choose No Layout. • Click OK.

4. Use the New Object tool to add: • Four **Mini-Borders.** • Four **Text** Blocks. • Four **Graphic** Blocks. Stretch and position each mini-border to its own corner of the page, as shown in the illustration. Do the same for each graphic and text block, placing one of each inside the four mini-borders. Use the illustration to guide you.

5. Edit mini-border 1: • Double-click block. • Choose Balloons. • Click OK.

6. Edit graphic block 1: • Double-click block. • Choose PSDeluxe Calendar Icons, Balloon. • Click OK.

7. Edit text block 1: • Double-click block. • **Font:** Paramount, **Size:** 96-point, **Style:** Bold on, **Justification:** Horizontal Center. • Type "B b". • Click OK.

8. Edit mini-border 2: • Double-click block. • Choose Diamond Corners. • Click OK.

9. Edit graphic block 2: • Double-click block. • Choose PSDeluxe Calendar Icons, Car Trip. • Click OK.

10. Edit text block 2: • Double-click block. • **Font:** Paramount, **Size:** 96-point, **Style:** Bold on, **Justification:** Horizontal Center. • Type "C c". • Click OK.

11. Edit mini-border 3: • Double-click block. • Choose Celtic. • Click OK.

12. Edit graphic block 3: • Double-click block. • Choose PSDeluxe Calendar Icons, Heart. • Click OK.

13. Edit text block 3: • Double-click block. • **Font:** Paramount, **Size:** 96-point, **Style:** Bold on, **Justification:** Horizontal Center. • Type "H h". • Click OK.

14. Edit mini-border 4: • Double-click block. • Choose Memo Planes. • Click OK.

15. Edit graphic block 4: • Double-click block. • Choose PSDeluxe Calendar Icons, Plane. • Click OK.

16. Edit text block 4: • Double-click block. • **Font:** Paramount, **Size:** 96-point, **Style:** Bold on, **Justification:** Horizontal Center. • Type "P p". • Click OK.

Other Ideas
For extra sturdiness, have your flashcards laminated, or glued to heavier cardboard or posterboard.

Other School Projects

Educational Worksheets

Creative worksheets are fun to make using your computer. Whether it's classroom games, activity pages, match-em-ups, or even coloring pages, your Print Shop version can help you design them all. Here's a PSD-DOS idea for a weekly review sheet.

1. Select: • Sign. • Create a New Project. • Tall.

2. Select a Backdrop: • Choose Sheep in Field. • Done.

3. Select a Layout: • Choose Sheep in Field 1.

4. Select Fill In or Edit.

5. Edit headline 1 (upper left corner): • Tab. • Font: Tubular. • Type "WEEKLY REVIEW", all capital letters. • Tab. • Done.

6. Edit headline 2 (cloud 2): • Tab. • Delete block. • Done.

7. Select Add New Elements; add: • Text Block. Place block where deleted headline was, stretch to fill cloud. Press Tab and Done when finished placing element.

8. Edit new text block: • Tab. • Font: New Zurica, Font Size: X-small. • Line Justify: Center, Placement: Center. • Tab. • Type worksheet instructions. • Tab. • Done.

9. Edit text block 2 (under new text block 1): • Tab. • Font: New Zurica, Font Size: 12-point. • Line Justify: Center, Placement: Center. • Tab. • Type worksheet question, such as "How many sheep are in this picture?" • Tab. • Done.

10. Edit text block 3 (2nd sheep): • Tab. • Font: New Zurica, Font Size: 12-point. • Line Justify:

Center, Placement: Center. • Tab. • Type another worksheet activity, such as multiplication problems to solve. • Tab. • Done.

11. Edit text block 4 (3rd sheep on left side): • Font: New Zurica, Font Size: 12-point. • Line Justify: Center, Placement: Center. • Tab. • Type another worksheet activity, such as scrambled words. • Tab. • Done.

12. Edit text block 5 (sheep on right side): • Tab. • Font: New Zurica, Font Size: 12-point. • Line Justify: Center, Placement: Center. • Tab. • Type another worksheet activity, such as history questions. • Tab. • Done.

13. Edit last headline block (at bottom of page): • Tab. • Font: Jester. • Tab. • Type "GOOD JOB! STUDY HARD!", or another positive message. • Tab. • Done.

Assignment Sheets

Organize your students with take-home assignment sheets to help them keep track of homework. Here's a sample sheet created on PSD-Windows.

1. Select: • **L**etterhead. • **S**ingle Page.

2. Select a Backdrop: • Choose Notebook. • Click OK.

3. Select a Layout: • Choose Notebook 1. • Click OK.

4. Edit headline block: • Double-click block. • **F**ont: Scribble. • Type "ASSIGNMENT SHEET", all capital letters. • Click OK.

5. Edit text block: • Double-click block. • **F**ont: Jester, Size: Medium, Justification: **H**orizontal Left. • Type individual assignments. • Click OK.

Use these steps to create a similar project on NPS:

1. Select: • Calendar. • Design Your Own. • Weekly. • Month. • Year. • Specific week.

2. Select Graphic: • Choose Full Panel. • Choose Library.

3. Select Message: • Choose Sierra, Solid. • Type "HOMEWORK ASSIGNMENTS", capital letters. • F10 to preview.

4. Select Middle of Calendar: • Now enter specific assignments or graphic for each day of the week.

Other Ideas The PSD Notebook backdrop also makes a wonderful page for kids, daily journals or diaries. Print out a copy and duplicate it to create a personal notebook.

ASSIGNMENT SHEET

History – read Chapter 4, fill in exercise 11 in your workbook.

Spelling – memorize your spelling list for quiz next Tuesday.

Math – practice your multiplication tables for test November 3rd.

English – read Chapter 5.

Turn in Field Trip permission slips for next week's trip to the Planetarium!

Other School Projects

Classroom Games

Your Print Shop program can help you add to the fun and excitement of classroom games. You can print out graphics, banners, and more. Here's an idea for a scavenger hunt game using a text book. Have the students look on specific pages of a text book to find answers to questions, and letters from the answers spell out a secret word. All the game instructions can be printed on an attractive sign project. Follow these PSD-DOS instructions to see an example.

1. Select: • Sign. • Create a New Project. • Tall.

2. Select a-Backdrop: • Choose Haunted House. • Done.

3. Select a-Layout: • Choose Haunted House 5.

4. Select Fill In or Edit.

5. Edit headline block: • Tab. • Font: PalatiaBold. • Tab. • Type "HAUNTED HOUSE HISTORY HINTS", all capital letters. • Tab. • Done.

6. Edit text block 1: • Tab. • Font: New Zurica, Font Size: 12-point. • Line Justify: Left, Placement: Top. • Tab. • Type game instructions and questions, for example: "PAGE 42: Find the name of the first President of the United States. Write the first letter of his first name in the first blank below." • Tab. • Done.

7. Edit text block 2: • Tab. • Font: New Zurica, Font Size: 12-point. • Line Justify: Center, Placement: Center. • Tab. • Type answer area: "Write the clue letters from above in order! _ _ _ _ _ Did you solve the mystery?" • Tab • Done.

Other Ideas   Design your own travel games, party games, or class games with your Print Shop program. You'll be surprised at the simple game sheets you can make: tic-tac-toe, hangman, scrambled words and pictures, memory games, and more. Browse through activity books to find ideas you can try!

Design Tips

Watch out for really small type. Cramming too much into a small space can make your design very difficult to read. Always avoid using a script front in a very small point size.

Program for School Play

Design a program to hand out to audience members at your next school play, recital, or concert. Create a front and back to be folded as this idea shows. Follow these PSD-Windows steps:

1. Select: • Sign. • Wide.

2. Select a Backdrop: • Choose Egyptian. • Click OK.

3. Select a Layout: • Choose Egyptian 1. • Click OK.

4. Edit headline block: • Double-click block. • Font: Stylus. • Type "Swim a Mile Up the Nile", or the name of your play. • Click OK. You may have to enlarge your block slightly.

5. Edit text block: • Double-click block. • Font: Paramount, Size: Medium, Justification: Horizontal Center. • Type names of cast members and production people. • Click OK.

Other Ideas   This is a project you can use for any special program where you want to list participants, topics, schedule of events, skits, etc. Design your own programs for seminars, recitals, trade shows, community meetings, or clubs.

Here are steps to create a similar program using NPS:

1. Select: • Sign or Poster. • Design Your Own. • Wide.

2. Select Graphic: • Choose Full Panel. • Choose Screen.

3. Select Message: • Choose Tiny, Solid. • Start your first line below the graphic; type your cast members names and parts. • F10 to preview.

Cue Cards

Use the sign project type to make cue cards for your school play. Follow these PSD-DOS steps to see how:

1. Select: • Sign. • Create a New Project. • Wide.

2. Select **A**dd New Elements; add: • Text-Block. Make one large text block to fill entire space. Press Tab and **D**one when finished placing element.

3. Edit text block: • Tab. • Font: New Zurica, Font Size: 42-point. • Line **J**ustify: Left, Placement: Top. • Tab. • Type in as many lines from the play as will fit on a page. • Tab. • **D**one. You may want to color-code the lines for each actor.

Cue Card Tip   Mount your cue cards to large posterboards—you can fit more to a board that way.

Follow these steps to create cue cards on your program version:

1. Select: • Sign or Poster. • Design Your Own. • Wide.

2. Select Message: • Choose a font like Amador or Madera to make your cue card messages. These fonts are easy to read from a distance, as long as you use a large font size.

JONES: Which way to the river, Smith?
SMITH: I think we should head toward that pyramid on the right.
JONES: I thought we just came from there?
SMITH: Hmmmm. Perhaps you're right, Jones. Maybe we're lost.
JONES: I knew this would happen.

Other Home Projects

With the capabilities of your Print Shop program, you'll find yourself coming up with hundreds of creations for use around the house. This next group of projects features ideas like family newsletters, allowance charts, recipe cards, and more. These ideas will use a variety of project types: letterhead, signs, greeting cards, and others. If you're at all unclear about the menu sequences for a particular home project, refer to previous parts pages in Section 3; they show the menus for creating that project type.

To help inspire you to create your own projects for the home, here's a list to spark your imagination:

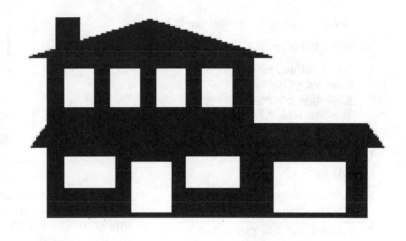

Phone lists

Address books

Videotape labels

Shopping lists

Drawer labels

Growth charts

Microwave instructions

Washing machine instructions

Emergency phone numbers

To Do lists

Games for rainy days

Family tree

Door signs

Placemats for the table

Notepads for the phone

Labels for books

Charts to track family

Award certificates for cleanest room

Family Newsletter

Newsletters are perfect for corresponding with family members, and they also make wonderful Christmas-card inserts. The project idea on this page shows you how to create a simple, one-page holiday newsletter using PSD-DOS.

1. Select: • Sign. • Create a New Project. • Tall.

2. Select a Layout: • Choose Sign 6.

3. Select Fill In or Edit.

4. Edit headline: • Tab. • Font: Subway. • Shape: Arc Up. • Shadow: Shape. • Colors, Shadow: Red. • Tab. • Type "HOLIDAY NEWS FROM THE BAKERS" (substitute your family name), all capital letters. • Tab. • Done.

5. Edit square graphic: • Choose Holiday Stamp. • Done.

6. Edit text block: • Tab. • Font: Jester, Font Size: 14-point. • Line Justify: Left, Placement: Center. • Frame: Thick Line. • Colors, Behind Text: Clear. • Tab. • Type your family news article, letter form. • Tab. • Done.

7. Edit row graphic (bottom): • Choose Nativity. • Done.

8. Select Add New Elements, add: • Square Graphic. Place graphic block over text block, matching size exactly. Press Tab and Done when finished placing graphic element.

9. Select Fill In or Edit.

10. Edit new graphic block: • Choose Biblical Angel. • Colors, Graphic: 40% Black. • Order: Send to Back. • Done.

Other Ideas If your newsletter needs more pages, just create a new sign project for each page needed. You can run them through a copier to print both sides of the newsletter paper. To use your newsletter as a mailer, create a design for the back of the newsletter that has three horizontal panels (tri-fold). The top two horizontal panels can have more newsletter articles and art. The bottom panel can be designed with room for a mailing label and a stamp.

Signs for Around the House

Use Print Shop signs to help family members remember chores and operate appliances, or simply leave them as notes. Sign projects are a breeze to design. Here's a great project idea for a sign to post by the microwave oven, with instructions telling how to operate it. Follow these simple PSD-Windows steps:

1. Select: • **S**ign. • **T**all.

2. Select a Backdrop: • Choose Blank Page. • Click OK.

3. Select a Layout: • Choose Sign 19. • Click OK.

4. Edit border: • Double-click border frame. • Choose Southwest border. • Click OK.

5. Edit headline: • Double-click block. • **F**ont: Librarian. • **S**hape: Receding. • Type "HOW TO WORK THE MICROWAVE", two lines, all capital letters. • Click OK.

6. Edit text block: • Double-click block. • **F**ont: NewZurica, **S**ize: Medium, **J**ustification: **H**orizontal Left. • Type the instructions for operating your oven; use numbered steps, upper- and lowercase letters. • Click OK.

Other Ideas   Create similar instruction signs for the washer, dryer, dishwasher, even for your computer!

Here are steps to create a similar sign using NPS:

1. Select: • Sign or Poster. • Design Your Own. • Wide.

2. Select Border: • Choose Wide. • Clipboard.

3. Select Message: • Choose Small, Solid. • Type your instructions, using numbered steps as illustrated.

Other Home Projects

Chore Charts

Keep track of chores with a handy list. To make a simple chart using the notepad orientation from the letterhead project type, follow the PSD-DOS steps included here.

1. Select: • Letterhead. • Create a New Project. • Notepad.

2. Select a Layout: • Choose Letterhead 12.

3. Select Fill In or Edit.

4. Edit bottom graphics blocks: • Choose Owl. • Apply to All: Yes. • Done.

5. Edit top left square graphic: • Choose Pushpin. • Done.

6. Edit text block 1: • Tab. • Font: Bazooka, Font Size: Large. • Frame: No Frame. • Tab. • Type "CHORE CHART," all capital letters. • Tab. • Done.

7. Edit text block 2: • Tab. • Font: NewZurica, Font Size: 32-point. • Frame: Thick Line. • Tab. • Type in your list of chores, numbered, upper- and lowercase letters. • Tab. • Done.

Other Ideas   Keep a master chore chart on a kitchen bulletin board or refrigerator to check off completed tasks.

Follow these steps to create an easy chore chart using NPS:

1. Select: • Sign or Poster. • Design Your Own. • Tall.

2. Select Border: • Thin. • Neon.

3. Select Graphic: • Small Corners. • Choose Graphics and select appropriate art for your chart.

4. Select Message: • Sierra, solid. • Type in your list and align to the left.

CHORE CHART

1. Take out the trash.
2. Feed the dog.
3. Clean your room.
4. Put dirty clothes in hamper.
5. Wash the dishes.
6. Mow the lawn.
7. Walk the dog.

Design Tip

To make a chart with blank lines to fill in later instead of typing in text, hold down the Shift key and the hyphen key (-) to draw lines across your text block.

Allowance Charts

Having trouble keeping track of everyone's allowance? Try this idea for making an allowance chart, using the weekly-calendar project type. Follow these PSD-Windows steps:

1. Select: • **Calendar.** • **Weekly.** • **Tall.** • Choose a year, month and specific week. • Click OK.

2. Select a Backdrop: • Choose Blank Page. • Click OK.

3. Select a Layout: • Choose Calendar 9. • Click OK.

4. Edit headline: • Double-click block. • **Font:** NewZurica. • **Shape:** Rectangular. • Type "ALLOW-ANCE CHART" and the name of the month, all capital letters. • Click OK.

5. Edit graphic block: • Double-click block. • Choose Lovable Pup, or other graphic. • Click OK. • You may want to enlarge the block slightly for a bigger graphic.

6. Edit calendar block: • Double-click block. • Edit each day to which you want to add text or a graphic; use the illustration as an example. • **Font:** Tubular, **Size:** Large **Justification:** Horizontal Center. • Click OK.

Use these steps to create a similar project on NPS:

1. Select: • Calendar. • Design Your Own. • Weekly. • Month. • Year. • Specific week.

2. Select Graphic: • Choose Full Panel. • Choose Houses.

3. Select Message: • Choose Sierra, Solid. • Type "ALLOWANCE CHART," capital letters. • F10 to preview.

4. Select Middle of Calendar: • Now enter specific chores to be done on each day that will earn an allow-ance.

Shopping Lists

Printed lists are helpful for tracking errands or shopping that needs to be Done. Here's a handy project idea for custom-making your own shopping list using PSD-DOS.

1. Select: • Letterhead. • Create a New Project. • Notepad.

2. Select a **B**ackdrop: • Choose Butterflies. • **D**one.

3. Select a **L**ayout: • Choose Butterflies 4.

4. Select **F**ill In or Edit.

5. Edit border: • Choose Double Line. • **D**one.

6. Edit headline: • Tab. • **F**ont: Heather. • Tab. • Type "SHOPPING LIST," capital letters. • Tab. • **D**one.

7. Select **A**dd New Elements; add: • Two **T**ext Blocks. Place two text blocks in middle of space, as shown in example, side by side. Press Tab and **D**one after placing each element.

8. Select **F**ill In or Edit.

9. Edit text block 1: • Hold down the Shift key and the hyphen key (-), and make lines from top to bottom of block. • Tab. • **D**one.

10. Edit text block 2: • Tab. • Hold down the Shift key and the hyphen key (-), and make lines from top to bottom of block. • Tab. • **D**one.

Gift Idea   Design a special shopping list project for a friend or family member. Take your design to a professional printer, and have it made into an actual notepad.

Recipe Cards

You'll have plenty of fun whipping up your own recipe cards with your Print Shop program. You can custom-design cards to fit any recipe book you have at home. Or make a special set of cards to give away as gifts. The following PSD-Windows steps show you how to design a card of your own.

1. Select: • **Letterhead.** • **Notepad.**

2. Select a Backdrop: • Choose Blank Page. • Click OK.

3. Select a Layout: • Choose No Layout. • Click OK.

4. Use the New Object tool to add: • **Square Graphic.** • **Text Block.** Just use the top half of the Notepad project space. Enlarge the square graphic to fill the upper half of the project space. Place the text block inside the graphic block and fill space as shown in illustration.

5. Edit square graphic: • Double-click block. • Choose PSDeluxe Initial Caps, Decor. • Click OK.

6. Edit text block: • Double-click block. • **Font:** Chaucer, **Size:** Small, Justification: Horizontal Center. • Type your recipe title. • **Font:** Librarian, **Size:** X-small. • Type your recipe instructions. • Click OK.

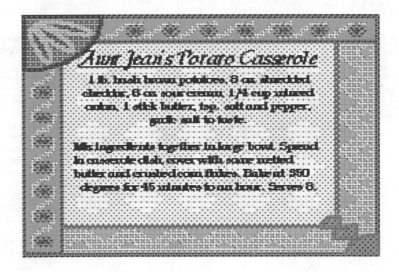

Other Ideas To protect your recipe cards, laminate them or place them in plastic covers. Also try gluing them to index cards; punch holes at the top or side of the cards, and keep them in a ring-binder. This also makes a great gift!

Other Home Projects

Phone Lists

Design your own phone directory using Print Shop. Or make a list of important numbers to keep by the phone. Use these PSD-DOS steps to help you.

1. Select: • Letterhead. • Create a New Project. • Notepad.

2. Select a **Layout**: • Choose Letterhead 18.

3. Select **F**ill In or Edit.

4. Edit column graphic: • Choose Herbs. • You may want to enlarge the graphic block to make bigger art. • **D**one.

5. Switch the locations of the two text blocks. Select the bottom block, Tab and **M**ove to top of project, select **D**one. Select the top block, Tab and **M**ove to bottom of project, select **D**one.

6. Edit top text block: • **F**ont: StageCoach. • Line **J**ustify: Center, **P**lacement: Center. • Frame: Thick Line. • **C**olors, Behind Text: 100% Yellow. • Tab. • Type "PHONE LIST," capital letters. • Tab. • **D**one.

7. Edit bottom block: • Tab. • **F**ont: Moderne, Font **S**ize: 16-point. • Line **J**ustify: Center, **P**lacement: Center. • Tab. • Type in your own names and phone numbers. • Tab. • **D**one.

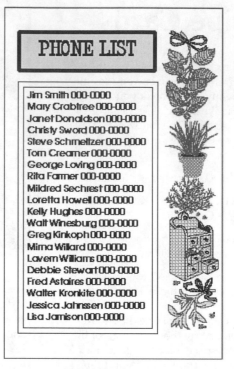

Other Ideas   Type up your entire phone list or mini-directory and enclose in a 3-ring binder. Design an attractive cover sheet too! If you save your phone list files, you can easily update them on your computer if anyone moves or changes numbers.

Address Books

Make your own address book to keep or give as a gift. You can even type in addresses before printing your book. Follow these PSD-Windows steps for a good example:

1. Select: • Letterhead. • Notepad.

2. Select a Backdrop: • Choose Blank Page. • Click OK.

3. Select a Layout: • Choose No Layout. • Click OK.

4. Use the New Object tool to add: • **Square Graphic.** • **Text Block.** Position the square graphic in upper left corner, size to fill entire project. Position text block inside graphic block and size to fill inner space.

5. Edit square graphic: • Double-click block. • Choose PSDeluxe Initial Caps, French. • Click OK.

6. Edit text block: • Double-click block. • **Font:** NewZurica, Style: Bold on, Size: Small, Justification: Horizontal Center. • Type in your addresses (if you're designing a book for a gift, type in blank lines). • Click OK.

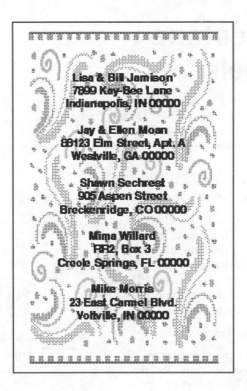

Design Tip

Don't forget to add color to your projects. Use markers, paints, or colored pencils to give your projects greater appeal.

Videotape Labels

Tired of using those boring old stick-on labels on your videotapes? Design your own fun labels with your Print Shop version. Follow these PSD-DOS steps to see how:

1. Select: • Letterhead. • Create a New Project. • Notepad.

2. Select Add New Elements, add. • Square Graphic. • Text Block. Use upper half of Notepad project space. Size graphic block to fill upper half of project. Place text block inside graphic. Press Tab and Done after placing elements.

3. Select Fill In or Edit.

4. Edit square graphic: • Tab. • Choose Other Libraries, Calendar, Television. • Done.

5. Edit text block: • Tab. • Font: NewZuricaBold, Font Size: Small. • Colors, Text: White. • Tab. • Type your videotape label, capital letters. • Tab. • Done.

Try making your labels using the greeting-card project type. Repeat your design on the inside of the card, and you'll get two labels to print out on one sheet.

1. Select: • Greeting Card. • Design Your Own. • Top Fold.

2. Select Graphic: • Choose Full Panel. • Choose Screen.

3. Select Message: • Choose Small, Solid. • Start typing below the graphic: type the name of the movie or TV show that's on the videotape you want to label. • F10 to preview.

4. Select Inside of Card: • Repeat steps 2 and 3.

Children's Growth Chart

Are your little monsters growing like weeds? Use the banner project to create a fun chart to track your child's growth. Follow these PSD-Windows steps:

1. Select: • **B**anner. • Vertical.

2. Select a Backdrop: • Choose Ogre. • Click OK.

3. Select a Layout: • Choose Ogre 5. • Click OK.

4. Edit headline block 1: • **F**ont: Subway. • Type your child's name. • Click OK.

5. Edit headline block 2: • **F**ont: NewZurica, Style: Bold on. • Type "GROWTH CHART," two lines, capital letters. • Click OK.

Chart Tip Keep track of each month's growth by measuring your child's height against the chart. Mark each recording with a colorful marker.

Font Tip If you're using a script font for your projects, avoid using all capital letters. Script fonts look best with both upper- and lowercase letters.

Follow these steps to create a similar banner:

1. Select: • Banner. • Design Your Own. • Vertical.

2. Select Graphic: • Choose Full Panel, Both Ends. • Choose Robot.

3. Select Message: • Choose Amador, Solid. • Type your child's name. • Press F10 to preview.

Other Projects & Crafts

This next group of projects will give you even more ideas for using your Print Shop program. You'll find projects for your church, club, or community organizations, as well as more crafty things you can do with your computer. These ideas will use a variety of project types: letterhead, signs, greeting cards, and others. If you're at all unclear about the menu sequences for a particular project shown, refer to previous parts pages in Section 3 that show the menus for creating that project type.

Here's a list of other project and computer craft ideas to further inspire you:

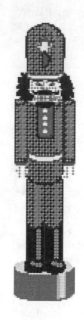

Club newsletters

Programs for special events

Club cards

Certificates and awards

Journals and personal calendars

Labels for luggage

Travel itineraries

Church newsletters

Brochures

Membership cards

Resumés

Labels for canning and jars

Decorations for gift boxes

Travel journals

Church Newsletter

Use newsletters to communicate upcoming events, interesting articles, special activities, and more. The project idea on this page shows you how to create a simple, one-page newsletter using PSD-Windows.

1. Select: • Sign. • Tall.

2. Select a Backdrop: • Choose Blank Page. • Click OK.

3. Select a Layout: • Choose Sign 16. • Click OK.

4. Switch the headline block and the ruled line block around. Move the headline to the top of the page, and the ruled line below the headline.

5. Edit headline: • Double-click on block. • Font: Sherwood, Style: Drop Shadow on. • Shape: Top Arch. • Type the name of your church, capital letters. • Click OK.

6. Edit ruled line 1: • Double-click block. • Choose Scotch. • Click OK.

7. Use the New Object tool to add a small text block between the headline and the ruled line, as shown in illustration.

8. Edit newly-added text block: • Double-click block. • Font: Moderne, Size: Medium, Justification: Horizontal Center. • Type the address of your church, upper- and lowercase letters. • Click OK.

9. Edit text block on left side of page: • Double-click block. • Font: NewZurica, Size: 14-point, Justification: Horizontal Left. • Type your newsletter article, upper- and lowercase letters. • Click OK. • Use the Frame tool to select a Thin Line frame.

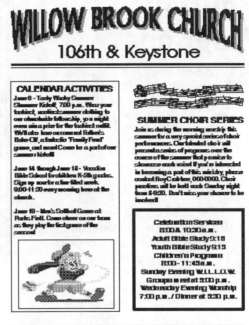

10. Edit text block on right side of page: • Reduce the size of the block, as shown in illustration, allowing room from newly-added square graphic above. • Double-click on block. • Font: NewZurica, Size: 14-point, Justification: Horizontal Left. • Type your newsletter article, upper- and lowercase letters. • Click OK.

11. Use the New Object tool to add extra graphics blocks and text blocks as needed. Study the illustration for examples.

12. Edit bottom ruled line: • Double-click block. • Choose Scotch. • Click OK.

Other Projects & Crafts

Church Programs

You can design your own programs for special musical presentations, plays, and other events using your Print Shop program . Follow these steps to design a program using PSD-DOS:

1. Select: • Sign. • Create a New Project. • Wide.

2. Select a **B**ackdrop: • Choose Three Wise Men. • **D**one.

3. Select **A**dd New Elements, add: • **B**order. • **H**eadline Block. • Two Text Blocks. Place headline across top of sign, stretch as shown in illustration. Place one text block to left of project, and size as shown in illustration. Place the other text block to the right of project. Press Tab and **D**one after adding elements.

4. Select Fill In or Edit.

5. Edit headline block: • Tab. • F**o**nt: Chaucer. • **S**hadow: Drop Shadow. • **S**hape: Arc Up. • Tab. • Type "A Christmas Cantata", or the name of your program, upper- and lowercase letters. • Tab. • **D**one.

6. Edit text block 1: • Tab. • F**o**nt: Chaucer, Font **S**ize: 16-point. • Line **J**ustify: Center, **P**lacement: Center. • **C**olors, Behind Text: White. • Tab. • Type in the names of the cast or performers. • Tab. • **D**one.

7. Edit text block 2: • Tab. • F**o**nt: NewZurica, Font **S**ize: 14-point. • Line **J**ustify: Center, **P**lacement: Center. • **F**rame: Thin Line. • **C**olors, Behind Text: White. • Tab. • Type in the names of the behind-the-scenes help, upper- and lowercase letters. • Tab. • **D**one.

8. Edit border: • Choose Joined Lines. • **D**one.

Design Tip

The steps just outlined create an interior to your program. Don't forget to make a cover design to print on the outside of your program. Have your programs printed through a copier on both sides (cover and interior).

Club Membership Forms

Your Print Shop program can be used to design all kinds of forms. Here's a project idea for a membership form for your club or organization. Follow these PSD-Windows steps:

1. Select: • **Letterhead.** • **Notepad.**

2. Select a Backdrop: • Choose Blank Page. • Click OK.

3. Select a Layout: • Choose Notepad 12. • Click OK.

4. Edit top left square graphic block: • Double-click block. • Choose Hockey. • Click OK.

5. Edit text block 1: • Double-click block. • **F**ont: Boulder, **S**ize: 16-point. • Type "ALL AMERICAN SPORTS CLUB", capital letters. • Click OK. • Select the Frame tool and add a Thin Line frame. • Select the Color palette and choose Yellow behind text.

6. Edit text block 2: • Double-click block. • Type up your membership form with lines for name, address, phone number, and other information needed. • **F**ont: NewZurica, Font Size: Small (Underline title of form). • **J**ustification: **H**orizontal Full. • Click OK.

7. Edit five square graphics at bottom: • Double-click on each block, and select a different sport graphic for each; Baseball, Basketball, Football, Soccer, Tennis. • Click OK.

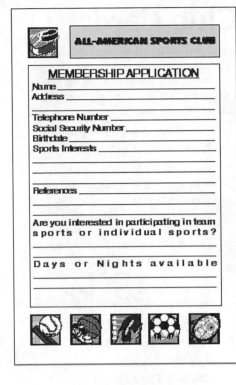

Design Tip

Remember, a notepad project will print out two to a page—so you'll have two of the same form to use.

Other Projects & Crafts

Club Cards

Make your own club membership cards with your Print Shop program. The idea on this page is a club card given out by a dentist. Use these PSD-DOS steps to see how it was made:

1. Select: • Letterhead. • Create a New Project. • Notepad.

2. Select Add New Elements, add: • Mini-Border. • Headline. • Text Block. • Square Graphic. Use upper half of Notepad project. Place headline at top, size as shown. Place text block below headline on left. Place square graphic beside text block, on right. Place mini-border around elements. Press Tab and Done when finished.

3. Select Fill In or Edit.

4. Edit mini-border: • Choose Blue Check. • Done.

5. Edit headline block: • Tab. • Font: Heather. • Shape: Arc Up. • Tab. • Type "BRIGHT SMILES CLUB", capital letters. • Tab. • Done.

6. Edit text block: • Tab. • Font: NewZurica, Font Size: 16-point. • Line Justify: Center, Placement: Center.• Tab. • Type: "This card certifies that the bearer is in good standing with his/her dentist for taking good care of his/her teeth.", upper- and lowercase letters. • Tab. • Done.

7. Edit square graphic: • Choose Happy Tooth. • Done.

Other Ideas   For a more professional look, have a professional printer print your finished cards on stiffer paper, or have them laminated.

Although you won't be able to duplicate exactly the project shown, here are some alternative steps using NPS:

1. Select: • Greeting Card. • Design Your Own. • Top Fold.

2. Select Graphic: • Choose Small Centered. • Graphics, Ribbon.

3. Select Customize and move the graphic to the lower right corner.

4. Select Message: • Choose Small, Solid. • Type the same message as shown in the PSD-DOS project.

Club Newsletter

Every member of your club will be impressed with your professional-looking newsletters. Design your newsletter to include information about upcoming events, interesting articles, club meetings, and more. The project idea on this page shows you how to create a simple, one-page newsletter using PSD-DOS.

1. Select: • Sign. • Create a New Project. • Tall.

2. Select a Layout: • Choose Sign 22.

3. Select Fill In or Edit.

4. Edit square graphic: • Tab. • Move graphic to left side of page and enlarge slightly. • Rotate, 0 degrees. • Frame: No Frame. • Tab. • Choose Running Computer. • Done.

5. Select Add New Elements, add: • Headline. • Text Block. • Horizontal Ruled line. Place headline at top of page, beside square graphic and size as shown in example. Place text block below headline. Place ruled line below text block. Press Tab and Done when finished placing elements.

6. Edit headline block: • Tab. • Font: NewZurica. • Shape: Round Top. • Tab. • Type "BEDFORD FALLS COMPUTER CLUB", two lines, capital letters. • Tab. • Done.

7. Edit new text block added: • Tab. • Font: Moderne, Font Size: 16-point. • Line Justify: Center, Placement: Center. • Tab. • Type your club's address, two lines, upper- and lowercase letters. • Tab. • Done.

8. Edit new ruled-line block: • Choose Scotch. • Done.

9. Edit left text block column: • Tab. • Font: NewZurica, Font Size: 14-point. • Line Justify: Full, Placement: Center. • Frame: Thin Line. • Tab. • Type in your newsletter article. • Tab. • Done.

10. Edit right text block column: • Tab. • Font: NewZurica, Font Size: 14-point. • Line Justify: Full, Placement: Center. • Tab. • Type in your newsletter article. • Tab. • Done.

11. Select Add New Elements, add: • Square Graphic. Place block at bottom right corner of column, as shown. Press Tab and Done.

12. Select Fill In or Edit.

13. Edit square graphic: • Choose Floppy Disks 5.25. • Done.

14. Edit bottom ruled line: • Choose Scotch. • Done.

Other Ideas

You can also try designing a side fold newsletter by using the wide orientation of the sign project type. Design one page with a front on the right side of the sign, and a back on the left side of the sign. Design another sign page with the interior layout of your newsletter.

Certificates and Awards

Use the sign project type to design certificates and awards to recognize outstanding individuals or achievements. The following PSD-Windows ideas show how to make an award for a club member.

1. Select: • **Sign.** • **Wide.**

2. Select a Backdrop: • Choose American Flag. • Click OK.

3. Select a Layout: • Choose No Layout. • Click OK.

4. With the New Object tool, add: • **Border.** • **Headline.** • **Text Block.** Place headline at top, size as shown. Place Text block below headline, fill remaining space.

5. Edit border: • Double-click block. • Choose Diamond Corners, Wide. • Click OK.

6. Edit headline: • Double-click block. • **Font:** Sherwood. • **Shape:** Arc Up. • Type "Citizen of the Year", upper- and lowercase letters.• Click OK.

7. Edit text block: • Double-click block. • **Font:** Calligrapher, **Size:** 38-point, **Justification:** **H**orizontal Center. • Type "Awarded to Barry Childs-Helton for outstanding community service above and beyond the call of duty. January, 1995", substituting your recipient's name, six lines, upper- and lowercase letters. • Click OK.

Here are steps to create a similar certificate using NPS:

1. Select: • Sign. • Design Your Own. • Tall.

2. Select Graphic: • Choose Full Panel. • Certif.

3. Select Message: • Choose Small, Solid. • Type your certificate message, starting your line below the art.

Resumé

You can even design a professional-looking resumé using your Print Shop program! Here's a simple one-page resumé designed on PSD-DOS.

1. Select: • Letterhead. • Create a New Project. • Regular.

2. Select a Layout: • Choose Letterhead 20.

3. Select Fill In or Edit.

4. Edit ruled line: • Choose Scotch. • Done.

5. Edit text block 1: • Tab. • Font: NewZuricaBold, Font Size: 12-point. • Tab. • Type your name, address, and phone number on four lines, upper- and lowercase letters. • Tab. • First line, Line Justify: Full. • Other three lines, Line Justify: Center. • Done.

6. Edit text block 2: • Type in your resumé information; career objective, education, work experience. • Tab. • Try using Font: NewZurica, Font Size: 12-point. • Line Justify: Left, Placement, Full. • Underline any headings. • Done.

Resumé Tip Use a better paper stock for printing your resumé. Remember to check for misspellings or typos before printing it out!

Design Tip

The best looking resumés are simple in design. You'll find layouts #10, 14, 15, and 20 ideal for making resumés.

Programs for Special Events

Is your club or community having a special event? Design a program to hand out to participants. With your Print Shop program and the wide sign project type, you can design a cover and an interior on both sides of one sheet of paper. Fold the paper, and you've got an instant program or brochure! Have the program printed up in large quantities. Here's a simple, elegant program cover idea using PSD-Windows.

1. Select: • **S**ign. • **W**ide.

2. Select a Backdrop: • Choose Blank Page. • Click OK.

3. Select a Layout: • Choose No Layout. • Click OK.

4. With the New Object tool, add: • Two **R**ow Graphics. • **H**eadline. • **T**ext Block. Place the row graphics at top and bottom, stretching across project. Place Headline on right side, middle. Place text block below headline, as shown in illustration.

5. Edit row graphic 1: • Double-click block. • Choose Bright Shapes. • Click OK.

6. Edit row graphic 2: • Double-click block. • Choose Bright Shapes. • Click OK. • Fli**p** both horizontally and vertically.

7. Edit headline: • Double-click block. • **F**ont: Boulder. • **S**hape: Double Arc Up. • Type "COMMUNICATIONS SEMINAR", capital letters. • Click OK.

8. Edit text block: • Double-click block. • Type "presented by TelePark Com Thursday, April 9 and Friday, April 10", four lines, upper- and lowercase letters.

• Font: NewZurica, Size: X-small, Justification: Horizontal Center for lines 1, 3 and 4. • Font: NewZurica, Style: Bold on, Size: Small for line 2. • Click OK.

You won't be able to create exactly the same project shown here. But here's an idea using your program:

1. Select: • Sign. • Design Your Own. • Wide.

2. Select Graphic: • Choose Small Rows II. • Graphics, Computer.

3. Select Message: • Choose Tiny, Solid. • Type your seminar title and dates, as shown above, but start your line below the graphics on your screen.

Journal

Create your own journal with a design from the Print Shop programs. You can even type in your entries right on screen and file them. Here's a simple journal page design created with the notepad orientation from the letterhead project type. This prints out two designs to a page. Follow these PSD-DOS instructions.

1. Select: • Letterhead. • Create a New Project. • Notepad.

2. Select **A**dd New Elements; add: • **C**olumn Graphic. • **H**eadline. • **H**orizontal Ruled Line. • **T**ext Block. Place Column graphic on left, size as shown. Place headline at top. Place ruled line beneath headline. Place text below ruled line and fill remaining space. Press Tab and **D**one when finished.

3. Select **F**ill In or Edit.

4. Edit column graphic: • Choose Pillar. • **D**one.

5. Edit headline block: • Tab. • **F**ont: Sherwood. • **S**hape: Rectangle. • Tab. • Type "DAILY JOURNAL", all capital letters. • Tab. • **D**one.

6. Edit ruled line: • Choose Flower Vine. • **D**one.

7. Edit text block: • Tab. • **F**ont: NewZurica, Font **S**ize: Medium. • Tab. • Hold down the Shift key and the hyphen (-) key to make lines throughout the block. • Tab. • **D**one.

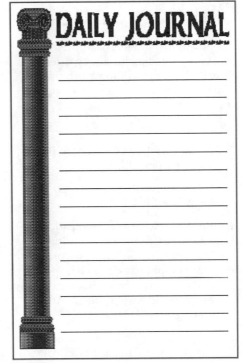

Here's a similar journal design you can try using NPS.

1. Select: • Sign or Poster. • Design Your Own. • Tall.

2. Select Border: • Choose Wide. • Columns.

3. Select Message: • Choose Lassen, Solid. • Type "DAILY JOURNAL", and then add dashes to create lines to write your entry.

Garden Labels

Using the notepad letterhead project type, you can make designer garden labels for your green-thumb activities. Follow these PSD-Windows steps to see how:

1. Select: • **L**etterhead. • **N**otepad.

2. Select a Backdrop: • Choose Blank Page. • Click OK.

3. Select a Layout: • Choose No Layout. • Click OK.

4. With the New Object tool, add: • **S**quare Graphic. • **T**ext Block. Use upper half of Notepad project. Place graphic block to fill upper half of project space. Place text block inside graphic block. After editing, adjust sizes.

5. Edit square graphic: • Double-click block. • Choose PSDeluxe Initial Caps, Victorian. • Click OK.

6. Edit text block: • Double-click block. • **F**ont: Chaucer, Size: 14-point, Justification: **H**orizontal Center. • Type "Violets", or the names of your particular garden plants, lowercase letters. • Click OK.

Other Ideas   Attach your printed and trimmed label to a sturdy piece of cardboard. Cover it with see-through plastic, or laminate to protect it from the elements. These labels can be stapled to sticks or wire posts, and placed near each plant or garden row.

Design Tip

You can probably fit another label below the one you designed following the steps just outlined. And remember, the notepad orientation prints out two to a page!

Labels for Luggage, Wallets, Purses

Here's a great idea for making sure your luggage, wallet, or purse has identification. Make labels with your name and address, using your Print Shop program. Follow these easy PSD-DOS steps:

1. Select: • Letterhead. • Create a New Project. • Notepad.

2. Select Add New Elements, add: • Row Graphic. • Text Block. Use upper portion of Notepad project space. Place row graphic at very top and text block on top of row graphic. Press Tab and Done when finished.

3. Select Fill In or Edit.

4. Edit row graphic: • Choose Blue Blend. • Done.

5. Edit text block: • Tab. • Font: NewZuricaBold, Font Size: 20-point. • Line Justify: Left. • Tab. • Type your name and address on three lines, upper- and lowercase letters. • Done.

Marsha Washington
908 Twelve Oaks Lane
Sacramento, CA 00000

You can also create labels using the Greeting Card, Sign or Poster, or Letterhead project types. For larger labels, use the Letterhead graphics and small or tiny text. Here's a project example:

1. Select: • Letterhead. • Design Your Own.

2. Select Graphic: • Full Panel. • Houses.

3. Select Text: • Tiny, Solid. • Type in label.

Design Tip

Repeat these design steps to fill the notepad page with labels. You'll find many uses for them, no matter how many you print to a page.

Other Projects & Crafts

Jar and Canning Labels

Personalize your handmade crafts, baked goods, or canned goods with creative labels designed on your computer. Use rubber cement or glue to attach your labels, or take them to a professional printer to have them made into stickers. Use these PSD-Windows project idea steps to see how:

1. Select: • Letterhead. • Notepad.

2. Select a Backdrop: • Choose Blank Page. • Click OK.

3. Select a Layout: • Choose No Layout. • Click OK.

4. With the New Object tool, add: • **S**quare Graphic. • **T**ext block. Use upper portion of Notepad project. Place square graphic at top, fill space as shown. Place text inside graphic. You may want to resize these blocks after you've filled them in. Press Tab and **D**one when finished placing elements.

5. Edit square graphic: • Double-click block. • Choose PSDeluxe Initial Caps, Scribble. • Click OK.

6. Edit text block: • Double-click block. • **F**ont: Jester, Size: 30-point, Justification: **H**orizontal Center. • Type "Aunt Nancy's Pickled Pears 9-7-94" (or the label for your project), upper- and lowercase letters. • Click OK. • Use the Frame tool to select a Drop Shadow frame. • Choose Color palette and select Behind Text 60% shaded Magenta.

Other Ideas   You'll find many uses for labels designed on your Print Shop program. Try identification labels, file labels, labels for your videotapes, drawer labels, garage tool labels, frozen food labels, lawn chair labels, book labels, and many more.

Decorative Paper for Gift Boxes

Paper-covered boxes of various sizes make wonderful gifts. Plain ones are available at craft stores, or you can use small boxes you have at home. They're fun to decorate and store keepsakes in. Here's a PSD-DOS idea for using your computer to make decorative paper to cover a special gift box, whether it's round or square. Simply print out a design you've created using your Print Shop program. Color it or paint it, then glue to your box and box lid. Add a ribbon or bouquet of dried or silk flowers, and you've got a crafty gift to give or keep for yourself.

1. Select: • Sign. • Create a New Project. • Wide.

2. Select **A**dd New Elements, add: • **S**quare Graphic.

3. Select **F**ill In or Edit.

4. Edit square graphic: • Tab. • Move block to upper left corner of page. • Stretch to fill entire space, as shown in illustration. • Tab. • Choose Other Libraries, Initial Caps, French. • **D**one.

Other Ideas You'll find many uses for the fancy designs from your Print Shop program: pretty shelf paper, sheets of stationery, placemats, and more. Browse through a paper craft book to find other uses around the house or for gift-giving.

You can also print out sheets of graphics: simply choose the sign project, and pick a graphic pattern that scatters art across the page. Choose a delicate drawing, like Daisies, and print!

Other Projects & Crafts

Postcards

Make your own personalized postcards to send. Follow the PSD-Windows steps below to make the illustration shown.

1. Select: • Greeting Card. • Top Fold.

2. Select a Backdrop: • Choose Crab on Beach. • Click OK.

3. Select a Layout: • Choose Crab on Beach #1. • Click OK.

4. Edit headline: • Double-click block. • Font: Subway, Justification: Horizontal Full. • Type "GREETINGS FROM FLORIDA!", two lines, capital letters. • Click OK.

5. Edit text block: • Double-click block. • Font: Jester, Size: 28-point, Justification: Horizontal Center. • Type "From just another crab on the beach", two lines, upper- and lowercase letters. • Click OK.

6. Edit border: • Leave border blank.

Other Ideas Children love receiving mail. Design some special child-oriented postcards for children in your local hospital, school, church, or for your own nieces, nephews, and cousins.

Design Tip

Print out your design, trim, and mount to heavy paper or cardboard. Don't forget to design the back of your card with a place to write a message.

Kid Stuff

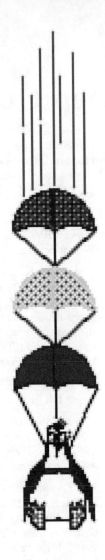

Hey, kids (and parents)! The projects in this next group are just for you. You can make all kinds of great kid projects with the Print Shop programs, including Keep Out signs, coloring books, holiday ornaments, and more. Make sure you have a parent or teacher around to help you follow the steps for each project and to get you started. These ideas will use a variety of project types: letterhead, signs, greeting cards, and others. If you're not sure how to use these project menus, look through the parts pages in Section 3.

Don't forget to color in your projects after you've printed them. Use crayons, markers, colored pencils, or paint. You can also use scissors and glue to add on to your creations. Be creative!

There's just not enough room in this book to show you all the neat projects you can make. But here's a list of some cool things you can try:

Storybooks	Board games	Lawnmowing signs
Address book	Diary or journal	Photo album
Flashcards	Gift wrap	Puzzles
School report covers	Travel games	Lunchbox stickers
Play money	Labels for your books	Play menus
Pictures to hang on your wall	Play order forms	Top Secret folders
Tickets	Play traffic tickets	Collection charts
Phony hall passes	Notebook covers	Pretend credit cards
Babysitting signs	Signs for your clubhouse	Banners for your room
Cards for your mom or dad	Banners for your science project	Award certificates
Book reports	Postcards to send to friends	Lemonade stand signs and banners
Sketchbook pads	Playing cards	Control panels for rocket ships

Keep Out Sign

Make a Keep Out sign that really works. Use your Print Shop program to design a sign for your door. Follow these PSD-DOS steps to see how:

1. Select: • Sign. • Create a New Project. • Tall.

2. Select a **B**ackdrop: • Choose Woodpecker. • Done.

3. Select **A**dd New Elements; add: • **H**eadline. • **T**ext Block. Place the headline at the top of the white space inside your backdrop. Place the text block underneath the headline and fill the remaining white space. Press Tab and **D**one after adding each element.

4. Select **F**ill In or Edit.

5. Edit headline block: • Tab. • **F**ont: Subway. • Tab. • Type "KEEP OUT!", two lines, capital letters. • Tab. • **D**one.

6. Edit text block: • Tab. • **F**ont: Boulder, Font **S**ize: 50-point. • Line **J**ustify: Center, **P**lacement: Center. • Tab. • Type "This means you!", three lines, upper- and lowercase letters. • Tab. • **D**one.

Sign Tip After your sign is printed, use crayons, markers or paint to color it in.

You won't be able to make the exact same sign, but here's an alternative to try using NPS:

1. Select: • Sign or Poster. • Design Your Own. • Tall.

2. Select Graphic: • Choose Reversed Diamond. • Choose Graphics, Folders, or another graphic you like.

3. Select Message: • Choose Madera, Solid. • Start typing below the art; type "TOP SECRET: KEEP OUT!", four lines, all capital letters.

Diary

You can make your own designer pages to put into a diary or journal. First design your page with lots of blank lines to write on. (If you use the notepad project from the letterhead type, you can print two diary designs on one page!) Print out several pages and trim them. You can punch holes in the sides and put them into a 3-ring binder to make your own diary book. Or you can staple a bunch together. Follow these PSD-Windows steps to make your design:

1. Select: • **Letterhead**. • **Notepad**.

2. Select a Backdrop: • Choose Blank Page. • Click OK.

3. Select a Layout: • Choose No Layout. • Click OK.

4. Use the New Object tool from the Tool Palette to add: • **Column** Graphic. • **Headline**. • **Text Block**. • **Square** Graphic. Place the column graphic on left side of page, stretch to fill space from top to bottom. Place headline at top of page. Place text block below headline and fill remaining space. Place square graphic at very bottom right corner, as shown in illustration.

5. Edit column graphic: • Double-click block. • Choose Hearts. • Click OK.

6. Edit headline block: • Double-click block. • **F**ont: Heather. • **S**hape: Pennant Right. • Type "MY DIARY", capital letters. • Click OK.

7. Edit text block: • Double-click block. • Hold down the Shift key and the hyphen key (-) to make lines throughout your block until it fills up. • Click OK.

8. Edit square graphic: • Choose Teddy. • Click OK.

Design Tip

Use your diary to write about things like: what happens to you each day, ideas that you might have, poems or stories, or you can even sketch things! Read through your diary from time to time to see what you've been up to.

Christmas Ornaments

You can make paper Christmas ornaments to hang on your tree. Design them on your computer, color them, and cut them out. Add ribbon or string to hang them. It's easy! The project idea on this page shows how to make three different kinds of ornaments using PSD-DOS.

1. Select: • Sign. • Create a New Project. • Tall.

2. For ornament 1, select **A**dd New Elements; add: • Two **S**quare Graphics. Place one graphic in upper left corner, stretch to size shown in illustration. Place second graphic inside first. You'll fill in the blocks in steps 4 and 5. Press Tab and **D**one after adding each block.

3. Select **F**ill In or Edit.

4. Edit square graphic 1: • Choose Other Libraries, Init Caps, Victorian. • **D**one.

5. Edit square graphic 2: • Tab. • Move block inside square graphic 1. • Stretch to fill inside of circle. • Tab. • Choose Other Libraries, PSD, Teddy. • **D**one.

6. For ornament 2, select **A**dd New Elements; add: • **S**quare Graphic. Place square graphic on left side of page and size as shown in illustration. Press Tab and **D**one when finished placing block.

7. Select **F**ill In or Edit.

8. Edit square graphic 3: • Choose Candy Cane. • Flip: Horizontal. • **D**one.

9. For ornament 3, select **A**dd New Elements; add: • **S**quare Graphic. • **M**ini-Border. Place square graphic in bottom left corner of page, size as shown in illustration. Place mini-border around square graphic. Press Tab and **D**one when finished.

10. Select **F**ill In or Edit.

11. Edit square graphic 4: • Choose Biblical Angel. • **D**one.

12. Edit mini-border: • Tab. • Stretch border to fit around angel, and place over graphic block. • Tab. • Choose Music, Large. • **D**one.

Other Ideas Glue on glitter, bows, and other holiday stuff to make your ornaments really special. It's also a good idea to glue your ornaments to cardboard or posterboard, and then cut them out. This will make them very sturdy.

Coloring Book

You can make your own coloring book or coloring pages using your Print Shop program. Find a graphic you like, enlarge it, print it out, and color! You can make several coloring pages and put them into a book. If you are using PSD, you can even print out coloring book outlines for all your art. Follow these PSD-Windows steps to make the coloring page shown in the illustration.

1. Select: • **Sign.** • **Tall.**

2. Select a Backdrop: • Choose Easter Basket. • Click OK.

3. Select a Layout: • Choose No Layout. • Click OK.

4. Select Print from the **F**ile menu. • Choose Coloring Book from the Print dialog box. • Click OK.

Other Ideas   Make a coloring book to give to a friend. Pick out your favorite square graphics and turn them into full page pictures following the steps above. When you've made a bunch, staple them together to make a book. Don't forget to design a cover for it!

You won't be able to find the exact same coloring page design, but here's another to try:

1. Select: • Sign or Poster. • Design Your Own. • Tall.

2. Select Graphic: • Choose Full Panel. • Choose Santa.

Kid Stuff

Puzzles

Print out your favorite picture and turn it into a puzzle. Use scissors to cut your picture into smaller shapes. Put the pieces into a decorated envelope, and give them to a friend to put together. Follow these PSD-DOS steps to make a giant picture.

1. Select: • Sign. • Create a New Project. • Tall.

2. Select **A**dd New Elements; add: • **S**quare Graphic. Place graphic in middle of page. Press Tab and **D**one when finished.

3. Select **F**ill In or Edit.

4. Edit square graphic: • Tab. • Move block to top left corner of page. • Stretch to fill entire page, as shown in illustration. • Tab. • Choose Pumpkin. • **D**one.

5. Print out your picture. Color it using crayons or markers. Cut the picture into shapes like puzzle pieces.

Here's a puzzle project for NPS:

1. Select: • Sign or Poster. • Design Your Own. • Tall.

2. Select Graphic: • Choose Large Top. • Choose Graphics, Desert, or another graphic you like.

3. Select Customize: • Enlarge the graphic and align it horizontally. To do this, press E, then the plus sign (+) on the keypad. Tapping the plus key enlarges your graphic. Press Enter when it's as large as it can get. To center it on the page again, press A, then H. You may have to do this several times to get a bigger graphic.

Storybook

Have you ever wanted to write your own storybook? Now you can, using your computer! First you must think of a story. Next, use your Print Shop program to make each page of your storybook. Look at the PSD-Windows steps below to see how we made a page from a storybook.

1. Select: • **S**ign. • **T**all.

2. Select a Backdrop: • Choose Sand Castle. • Click OK.

3. Select a Layout: • Choose No Layout. • Click OK.

4. Use the New Object tool from the Tool Palette to add: • **S**quare Graphic. • Two **T**ext Blocks. For now, place the blocks anywhere on the page. Follow steps 5–7 to see where to put the blocks and how big to make them.

5. Edit square graphic: • Move the block to the left side of the page. Size as shown in illustration. • Double-click block. • Choose PSDeluxe Initial Caps, Decor. • Click OK.

6. Edit text block 1: • Shrink the block and move it so it fits inside the graphic block. • Double-click block. • Font: Heather, Size: 68-point. • Type "O", capital letter. • Click OK.

7. Edit text block 2: • Move block beside square graphic. • Stretch to fill space, as shown in illustration. • Double-click block. • Font: Heather, Size: 30-point, Justification: **H**orizontal Left. • Type a paragraph from your story here. • Click OK.

You can create different pages for your book, just like the one you've just finished. You'll find lots of art to use to illustrate your story. If you can't find any art to go with your story, just print out the words, and draw your own picture on the page.

Other Ideas   Once you've finished your story, color in the pages. You can punch holes along the sides and put your storybook into a 3-ring binder. Now you've got a book to share with a friend or family member.

Memory Match-Up Game

You can make really neat memory-match game flashcards using the art on your Print Shop program. Make a set of cards, like the ones in the illustration. Print out two copies, so you have two of the same card. Cut them out and mix them up. Place them face down on a table or floor. Turn over one card, then turn over another to find the matching card. An instant game! Follow these PSD-DOS instructions to see how to make your cards:

1. Select: • Sign. • Create a New Project. • Wide.

2. Select **A**dd New Elements; add:
   • Four **S**quare Graphics. Place each graphic in a corner of the page and size as shown in illustration. If you're having trouble, just follow the sizing instructions in steps 4–7. Press Tab and **D**one after adding each block.

3. Select **F**ill In or Edit.

4. Edit square graphic 1: • Tab. • Move block to top left corner of page. • Stretch to fill top left corner, as shown in illustration. • Tab. • Choose Birthday Hippo. • **F**rame: Thick Line. • **D**one.

5. Edit square graphic 2: • Tab. • Move block to top right corner of page. • Stretch to fill top right corner, as shown in illustration. • Tab. • Choose Burger. • **F**rame: Thick Line. • **D**one.

6. Edit square graphic 3: • Tab. • Move block to lower left corner of page. • Stretch to fill lower left corner, as shown in illustration. • Tab. • Choose Leprechaun. • **F**rame: Thick Line. • **D**one.

7. Edit square graphic 4: • Tab. • Move block to lower right corner of page. • Stretch to fill lower right corner, as shown in illustration. • Tab. • Choose Spaceship. • **F**rame: Thick Line. • **D**one.

8. Print out two copies of your page. Cut apart the squares. Follow the instructions below to play.

To Play Memory Match-Up, mix up the squares and spread them out on the floor or table, face down. Now turn over one card. Remember what it looks like. Turn over another card to see if you can find a match to the first card. If it's a match, you can pick up the two cards. If it's not a match, turn them back over and let someone else have a turn. You and your friends can take turns playing this memory match-up game!

Other Ideas Try making a Puzzle Match-Up game using the cards you made. Cut each card into two pieces. Mix them up and turn them over on a table or floor. Turn over one piece. Now turn over another piece and see if they go together. If they do, you have a match and can pick up the cards. If they don't match, turn them back over and let someone else try.

Design Tip

To make your memory game harder, design more pages with different graphics, following the instructions above.

Flashcards

You can make flashcards to help you with math or language. Or you can make a set to help your little brother or sister. Follow these PSD-Windows steps to create some number flashcards.

1. Select: • **Sign.** • **Wide.**

2. Select a Backdrop: • Choose Blank Page. • Click OK.

3. Select a Layout: • Choose No Layout. • Click OK.

4. We're going to show you how to make the first flashcard. Then you can follow the same steps to create the other flashcards shown, or make up your own. Use the New Object tool from the Tool Palette to add: • **Text Block.** Place the block in the upper left corner and size to fill upper left corner, as shown in illustration.

5. Edit text block: • Double-click block. • **Font:** Boulder, **Size:** Extra Large, **Justification:** **H**orizontal Left. • Type "3". • Click OK.

6. Use the New Object tool to add a graphic block inside the text block: • Shrink the block to fit a small picture. • Double-click block. • Choose PSDeluxe Squares, Bunny. • Click OK.

7. To copy the other square graphics: • From the **E**dit menu, choose **C**opy. • Then from the **E**dit menu, choose **P**aste. • Now you should have two bunnies, but one is on top of the other. Click on the top bunny and move the block beside the first bunny. • To make bunny number 3, choose **P**aste from the **E**dit menu again. • Click the top bunny and move the block to fit under the other graphics. • Now you should have three bunnies.

You can even resize your art squares, make some large or small, or flip them horizontally. You can even rotate your rabbits!

Follow these same steps to create each flashcard shown. You can use any of the square graphics to make lots of copies of art.

Kid Stuff

Play Money

Have you ever wanted to design your own play money? Now you can with the Print Shop programs. Look at the PSD-Windows steps below to see how to make your own play money.

1. Select: • Letterhead. • Notepad.

2. Select a Backdrop: • Choose Blank Page. • Click OK.

3. Select a Layout: • Choose No Layout. • Click OK.

4. Use the New Object tool from the Tool Palette to add: • Two Square Graphics. • Two Text Blocks. • Headline. Place your blocks in empty spaces on your page. You'll size them and fill them in with steps 5–9.

5. Edit square graphic 1: • Move the block to the upper left corner of the page. • Stretch across page. • Double-click block. • Choose PSDeluxe Initial Caps, Stamp. • Click OK. • Choose Color palette and select Behind Object Green.

6. Edit square graphic 2: • Move block inside of graphic block 1 to the very middle. • You may have to enlarge this block slightly. • Double-click block. • Choose PSDeluxe Squares, New Year's Baby. • Click OK.

7. Edit headline: • Move block to top of graphic block 1. • Stretch across top, as shown in illustration. • Double-click block. • Font: Steamer. • Shape: Arc Up. • Type "PLAY MONEY", capital letters. • Click OK.

8. Edit text block 1: • Shrink the block and move it so it fits inside the graphic block on the left side of the New Year's Baby. • Double-click block. • Font: Boulder, Size: 68-point, Justification: Horizontal Center. • Type "$5". • Click OK.

9. Edit text block 2: • Shrink the block and move it so it fits inside the graphic block on the right side of the New Year's Baby. • Double-click block. • Font: Boulder, Size: 68-point, Justification: Horizontal Center. • Type "$5". • Click OK.

Design Tip

You've got room to make more money on your page. Repeat the steps above, but move your blocks to the empty places.

Play Menus

Are you opening up a play restaurant? You'll need play menus to use. Here's an easy idea for making a play menu using PSD-DOS.

1. Select: • Sign. • Create a New Project. • Tall.

2. Select a **B**ackdrop: • Choose Mode Cafe. • **D**one.

3. Select a **L**ayout: • Choose Mod Cafe 1.

4. Select **F**ill In or Edit.

5. Edit headline: • Tab. • Font: Jester. • Tab. • Type "Sally's Restaurant", or use your own name, upper- and lowercase letters. • Tab. • **D**one.

6. Edit text block 1: • Tab. • Font: Jester, Font **S**ize: Medium. • Tab. • Type your menu items, such as "Ham & Cheese Sandwiches, .75 Chips .50", three lines. • Tab. • **D**one.

7. Edit text block 2: • Tab. • Font: Jester, Font **S**ize: 40-point. • Style: Drop Shadow. • Tab. • Type "Ice Cream Sundaes, 1.50", three lines, upper- and lowercase letters. • Tab. • **D**one.

Follow these steps for a different kind of play menu project using NPS:

1. Select: • Sign or Poster. • Design Your Own. • Tall.

2. Select Graphic: • Choose Small frame. • Choose Graphics, Coffee or another graphic you like.

3. Select Message: • Choose Small, Solid. • Type in your menu items.

Play Order Forms

You can make all sorts of fun order forms to play with. Here's a project idea for making a order form notepad for your play restaurant. Follow these PSD-Windows steps:

1. Select: • Letterhead. • Notepad.

2. Select a Backdrop: • Choose Cupcakes & Candy. • Click OK.

3. Select a Layout: • Choose No Layout. • Click OK.

4. Use the New Object tool from the Tool Palette to add: • Two Text Blocks. Follow steps 5 and 6 to see where to place the blocks.

5. Edit text block 1: • Move block to top right corner of page. • Stretch to fit, as shown in illustration. • Double-click block. • Font: Bazooka, Size: Large, Justification: Horizontal Center. • Type "MAY I TAKE YOUR ORDER PLEASE?", upper- and lowercase letters. • Click OK.

6. Edit text block 2: • Move block below headline. • Stretch to fill open space, as shown in illustration. • Double-click block. • Hold down the Shift key and the hyphen key (-), and make lines throughout the block until you run out of room. • Click OK.

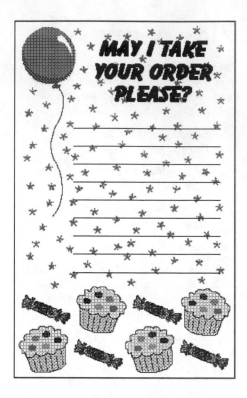

Design Tip

This project will print two to a page. Print out five pages, trim each form, and staple them together to make a notepad.

Lemonade Stand Banner

Make a giant banner for your next lemonade stand. You can design a banner that's sure to make everyone notice. Follow these PSD-DOS steps to make a cool lemonade stand banner:

1. Select: • Banner. • Create a New Project. • Horizontal.

2. Select a **B**ackdrop: • Choose Art Deco. • **D**one.

3. Select a **L**ayout: • Choose Art Deco 3.

4. Select **F**ill In or Edit.

5. Edit headline: • Tab. • **F**ont: Boulder, Font **S**ize: Small/Large. • Tab. • Type "FRESH-SQUEEZED LEMONADE .50", capital letters. • Tab. • **D**one.

Other Ideas Don't forget to make signs or flyers for your lemonade stand. Use the sign project type to help you.

Follow these steps for a different kind of banner:

1. Select: • Banner. • Design Your Own. • Horizontal.

2. Select Graphic: • Choose Full Panel on Both Ends. • Choose Saletag.

3. Select Message: • Choose Small Line Over Large, Amador, Solid. • Type "FRESH-SQUEEZED LEMONADE .50", capital letters, two lines, as shown in illustration.

Lawnmowing Sign

You'll drum up business all over the neighborhood with lawnmowing signs made with the Print Shop programs. Here's an easy sign you can make with PSD-Windows.

1. Select: • Sign. • Tall.

2. Select a Backdrop: • Choose Blank Page. • Click OK.

3. Select a Layout: • Choose Sign 15. • Click OK.

4. Edit headline: • Double-click block. • Font: Sherwood. • Shape: Arc Up. • Type "LAWN MOW-ING", capital letters. • Click OK. • Stretch the block to make it bigger, as shown in illustration.

5. Edit text block: • Double-click block. • Font: Boulder, Size: Large, Justification: Horizontal Center. • Type "CALL BILLY SPRAGUE 000-0000" (but use your own name and phone number), all capital letters. • Click OK.

6. Edit mini-border: • Double-click border. • Choose Geo. • Click OK.

Design Tip

If you're hanging your sign outside, you might want to cover it with clear plastic to protect it from the weather.

Babysitting Sign

Let everyone in your neighborhood know you're available to babysit. Post your signs on poles, or hand them out as flyers. Here's a simple sign you can make with PSD-DOS.

1. Select: • Sign. • Create a New Project. • Tall.

2. Select a **B**ackdrop: • Choose Gingerbread Man. • **D**one.

3. Select a Layout: • Choose Gingerbread Man 5.

4. Select **F**ill In or Edit.

5. Edit headline: • Tab. • **F**ont: Subway. • **S**hape: Arc Up. • Tab. • Type "BABYSITTING", capital letters. • Tab. • **D**one.

6. Edit text block 1: • Tab. • **F**ont: Subway, Font **S**ize: 40-point. • Line **J**ustify: Center, Placement: Center. • **C**olors, Behind Text: Clear. • Tab. • Type "CALL JENNY WEBSTER 000-0000" (but use your name and phone number), capital letters. • Tab. • **D**one.

7. Edit text block 2: • Tab. • **F**ont: Subway, Font **S**ize: Medium. • You may have to move the block left or right to fit in space. • Tab. • Type "References Available", two lines, upper- and lowercase letters. • Tab. • **D**one.

Other Ideas   Advertise your business by placing signs in doorways and mailboxes around your neighborhood.

Notebook Cover

Here's a nifty notebook cover idea using PSD-Windows. You can make different covers for all your school books!

1. Select: • **Sign.** • **Tall.**

2. Select a Backdrop: • Choose Ocean & Jungle. • Click OK.

3. Select a Layout: • Choose Ocean & Jungle 5. • Click OK.

4. Edit headline: • Double-click block. • **Font: Boulder.** • Type "ENGLISH CLASS," or the name of your class, capital letters. • Click OK.

5. Edit text block: • Double-click block. • **Font: New Zurica, Style: Bold on, Size: 28-point, Justification: Horizontal Center.** • Type your name, and the name of the class teacher. • Click OK.

Follow these steps for a different kind of cover:

1. Select: • **Sign or Poster.** • **Design Your Own.** • **Tall.**

2. Select Graphic: • Choose Reversed Diamond. • Choose Graphics, and pick a graphic you like.

3. Select Message: • Choose Small, Solid. • Type in your class title.

Design Tip

Don't forget to add color to your notebook cover. Crayons, markers, and paint can make your notebook cover a work of art. You might also try printing your project on colored paper. Make colorful covers for all of your class notebooks!

School Report Covers

Show your teacher how creative you can be with a cool report cover designed on your Print Shop program. Follow these PSD-DOS steps to create the project shown:

1. Select: • Sign. • Create a New Project. • Tall.

2. Select a **B**ackdrop: • Choose Egyptian Party. • **D**one.

3. Select a **L**ayout: • Choose Egyptian Party 1.

4. Select **F**ill In or Edit.

5. Edit headline block 1: • Tab. • **F**ont: Tribune. • Tab. • Type "HISTORY", capital letters. • Tab. • **D**one.

6. Edit text block 1: • Tab. • **F**ont: Stylus. • Line **J**ustify: Center, Placement: Center. • Tab. • Type the title of your report, upper- and lowercase letters. • Tab. • Done.

7. Edit headline block 2: • Type your name, two lines, upper- and lowercase letters. • Boulder. • Done.

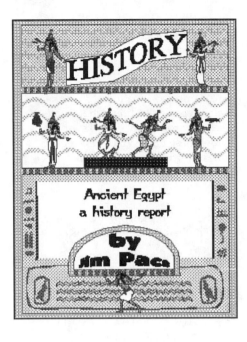

You can make report covers with the Letterhead project. Follow these steps to see how.

1. Select: • Letterhead. • Design your own.

2. Select Graphic: • Full Panel. • Library.

3. Select Text: • Choose a font you like and type in the title to your report.

You can also use the Sign project to make report covers too.

Collection Chart

Here's a project idea to help you keep track of your collection, whether it's baseball cards, stamps, rocks, or shells. Follow these PSD-Windows steps to make a chart for your football card collection:

1. Select: • Sign. • Tall.

2. Select a Backdrop: • Choose Football Field. • Click OK.

3. Select a Layout: • Choose Football Field 1. • Click OK.

4. Edit text block 1: • Double-click block. • Font: Bazooka, Size: Small. • Type "FOOTBALL CARD COLLECTION", capital letters. • Click OK. • Use the Frame tool to add a Thin Line frame.

5. Edit text block 2: • Double-click block. • Font: New Zurica, Size: Small, Justification: Horizontal Left. • Type the name of your card, team, date, and maker; use three lines, upper- and lowercase letters. • Click OK.

Other Ideas   If your collection uses several pages, punch holes in the sides and put them into a 3-ring binder. This will keep you really organized!

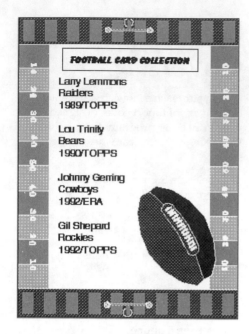

Text Tips

This section will give you some further information about using text in the Print Shop programs. You'll learn about different available fonts, how to work with the different sizes, how to edit your text blocks, and other text design tips that can improve your Print Shop projects.

Fonts

Fonts are the various styles of letters you can choose for your text. There are quite a variety of fonts available, ranging in looks from chunky and fat to handwritten and soft. In the world of professional printers, fonts are classified into two categories, *serif* and *sans serif*. These Latin-based words basically mean feet (serif) and without feet (sans serif). A typestyle like Paramount (PSD-DOS and Windows) or Sierra (NPS) has little feet or appendages that extend from the bottom of the character. (See Figure 4.1 for an example.) You're probably used to seeing this font style in newspapers and books. A typestyle like New Zurica (PSD-DOS and Windows) or Madera (NPS) does not have these appendages, instead each character is more block-like, see Figure 4.2. Block typestyles are more common in advertising (on billboards, for example).

In addition to the different fonts, there are different styles, or looks, available for each font. A font can be italicized, made bold, underlined, and more. See Figure 4.3 for some examples. These design options for changing the look of your text give you great flexibility in creating the perfect look for your project.

Sizes

Not only are fonts available in different styles, but they are also available in different sizes. These range from very large to very small. In the professional printing world, *point size* is the height of a font's characters, measured in points (one point equals 1/72 inch). Figure 4.4 shows some different point sizes.

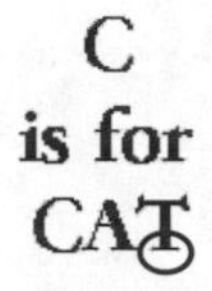

C
is for
CAT

Serif characters have feet.

D
is for
DOG

Sans-serif characters
do not have feet.

*Figure 4.1
An example of a serif
font.*

*Figure 4.2
An example of a
sans-serif font.*

Italics
Outline
Bold
Drop shadow
Mask

*Figure 4.3
Font design options
for PSD users
include italics,
outline, bold, drop
shadow, and mask.*

10 point size
18 point size
24 point size
36 point size

*Figure 4.4
Examples of point
sizes.*

The Print Shop programs offer several distinct size choices to use. If you're using NPS, the size is determined by font choice. For example, Amador is much larger than Madera. If either of these fonts is still too large for your text, try using *Small* or *Tiny* instead.

If you're using PSD for DOS or Windows, the size is chosen from a list that ranges from extra large to extra small. (See Figure 4.5.) But the list also offers you a chance to enter in a specific point size not covered by the size ranges. If you're having trouble getting your text block to fit in medium size, and small is too small, select Other at the bottom of the size list, and type a point size that is less than the medium size of 36-point. (Try 34, 32, and so on.)

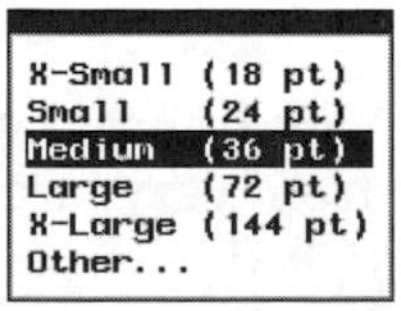

```
X-Small  (18 pt)
Small    (24 pt)
Medium   (36 pt)
Large    (72 pt)
X-Large (144 pt)
Other...
```

*Figure 4.5   The
size menu from
PSD, DOS version.*

Positioning

Now that you know a little more about fonts, you need to know the different ways of displaying your text. There are numerous ways of placing your text within your text block. Vertical positioning is called *placement* in the PSD programs (DOS and Windows). Placement can position text at the top of the block, in the center of the block, or at the bottom of the block. Horizontal positioning is called *justification* or *alignment*. Alignment is all text lines lined up at the left of the block, at the right of the block, centered in the block, or justified in the block. Figure 4.6 shows examples of each.

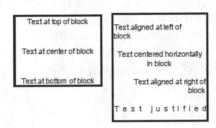

Figure 4.6 Examples of text positioning.

Justified text is text that is stretched out across the text block forming both a left-aligned and right-aligned margin. (This design option is not available if you use NPS.) Justified text can create some interesting text blocks, and is especially useful if you're doing a newsletter. Justified text is used frequently in newspapers and magazines.

How to Edit Text

You'll find many occasions for editing, or changing, your text block after you've typed in the words. For example, suppose you've misspelled a word. To make a correction using PSD (DOS or Windows), simply place the cursor where the edit needs to go, and delete the wrong character or add the correct letter. If you use NPS, you'll have to place the cursor on the line with the mistake, back up until you've reached the error, then retype the line.

If you use PSD for DOS or Windows, you'll be able to edit your text the way you do with a word processing program. This involves highlighting the word or words to be changed. For example, if there's a word in the middle of your text block that you want to stand out by choosing another typestyle, use the mouse or arrow keys to highlight the word. Here's how:

- Using the mouse, move the cursor to the word and double-click to highlight.

- Using the keyboard, move the cursor to the word with the arrow keys, hold down the Shift key, and press the arrow keys until the entire word is highlighted.

Once a word is highlighted, you can use the Edit box to choose a new typestyle. These same techniques can be used for entire blocks of text, changing sizes and styles, and controlling the position of the text. But remember, only what is highlighted will be changed.

If you're using PSD, you'll find additional editing options available in your edit box. The following descriptions will briefly tell what each one does. (These same options are available on PSD-Windows from the pull down menu bar or the Tool Palette.)

Done	Select this when finished editing (DOS only).
Colors	Lets you choose colors to use in your project. This is only useful if you have a color printer, or just want to see how different colors might look in your design. Using different colors on a monochrome printer will give you different intensities of black.
Frame	Lets you place a box around the text block. The menu gives you several frame styles to choose from.
Move	Lets you move a block and place it somewhere else on your project. (PSD-Windows, use the pointer from the Tool Palette to move blocks.)
Resize	Lets you make your block smaller or larger using the mouse or keyboard arrows. (PSD-Windows, use the pointer to click on a block corner, and drag the mouse to resize.)
Rotate	This comes in handy for type you want to tilt. It works the same way as rotating a graphic, as explained in Section 5. Just determine how many degrees to tilt your block.
Preview	Lets you preview how the text looks—font and size, and any special effects—immediately.
Order	Lets you position, or layer, a block in the foreground or background of your project (useful for placing text over a square graphic, for example). The backdrop is always considered

the back layer, and the border is always the front layer.

Undo Undoes your last action.

Delete Makes an entire block disappear.

Clear Text Empties your block of all text currently in it.

Select All Highlights everything in the text block making it easy to change fonts or sizes.

> *PSD-DOS, release 1.2* With the latest PSD release, you can now see a sample of the font before you choose it. When you select the Font option, you'll see an example at the top of the menu of the font that's highlighted.

NPS Text Editing

If you're using NPS, your editing commands appear in a Customize menu available after the initial project steps have been completed (see Figure 4.7). Most of the edit commands are the same as those listed for the PSD programs, worded differently. Many of these commands will not work on a text block unless you select Change Text to Graphic. This causes the block to be treated like a graphic element, to be moved, rotated, etc. Once a text block has been changed to a graphic block, it cannot be edited as text. *Warning: it can never be changed back to (and considered) a text block ever again!*

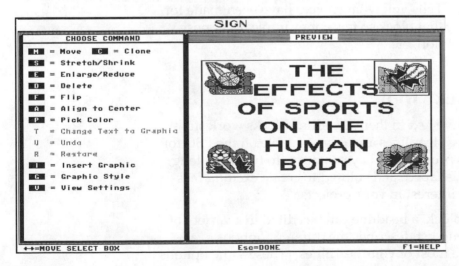

*Figure 4.7
NPS Customize
menu.*

Move	Lets you move the block.
Clone	Lets you copy a block; useful in creating symmetry in your project.
Stretch/Shrink	Lets you scale a block, such as making it elongated.
Enlarge/Reduce	Lets you resize a block proportionately.
Delete	Erases a block.
Flip	Lets you flip a block horizontally or vertically.
Align to Center	Lets you align the block within the project.
Pick Color	Allows you to choose a color for the block components.
Change Text to Graphic	Allows the system to treat a text block just like a graphics block.
Undo	Undoes your last action (except Change Text to Graphic).
Restore	Restores the earlier version of your project if you saved it before going into the Customize menu.
Insert Graphic	Lets you put another graphic block in.
Graphic Style	Lets you make special effects to graphics blocks similar to those available for text blocks, such as outline or shadow.
View Settings	Tells you what choices have been made for that block so far. For example, font, position, etc.

Headlines Are Text Too!

Because they have text in them, headline blocks work similarly to text blocks. Headlines are only available on the PSD for DOS or Windows programs. They can be up to two lines long, and can be styled, shaped, and colored to create exciting messages or points of interest in your projects.

Just like a text block, a headline can be edited in a variety of ways. The following list describes the different options available to making the most of your headlines. (These same options are available on PSD-Windows from the headline edit box, the pull down menu bar, or the Tool Palette.)

Colors   This command lets you choose colors (or shades of black and white) for the headline type. (These controls are found in the Color Palette for PSD-Windows.)

Font   Naturally, this lets you choose from a list of fonts.

Line Justify Controls how the headline is positioned: left, right, centered, or fully justified.

Style   In PSD-DOS this selection presents a variety of special effects to use, and it's especially fun to try them all! (These effects are controlled by the *Customize* command in PSD-Windows.) In PSD-Windows, the Style selection lets you use bold, italic, etc.

Shadow   Another stylistic design alternative to add different types of shadow effects to the headline. (This option is called *Customize* in the PSD-Windows Edit box.)

Shape   Lets you control how the headline is displayed in your project. You'll find numerous choices, from arches to angles.

Frame   Lets you place a box around the headline block.

Move   Allows you to move the block around.

Resize   Lets you enlarge or reduce the block.

Rotate   Lets you tilt the headline the same as rotating a graphic shown in Section 5.

Order   Lets you position, or layer, a block in the foreground or background of your project. This is useful for placing a headline over a square graphic, for example. However, the backdrop is always considered the back layer and the border is always the front layer.

Undo   Undoes your last action.

Delete   Makes an entire block disappear.

Clear Text   Empties your block of all text currently in it.

PSD-DOS, release 1.2   Several new features for headlines have been added. The first is an improvement in display speed. The previous version took a long time to draw headlines on your screen; release 1.2 solves this problem. The second new feature is the ability to control color shading to create special effects. The third is shapes. The shape menu option now shows the headline shapes next to the shape names in your menu list.

Text Design Tips

The following is a list of tips to apply when working with text in your projects.

- It's generally not a good idea to mix too many fonts together. Your project may end up looking too busy, distracting the reader from your message.

- Not all styles work well for all fonts (outline, for example). If you were using PSD and chose Standout font, it wouldn't look very appealing to choose the outline style to apply, since the font is already outlined.

- When using a script font, such as Signature (PSD) or Merced (NPS), try to avoid using all capital letters. The idea behind a script font is to look handwritten in cursive style. Most of us would never write our cursive in all capital letters, because it breaks the flow of the style. The same applies to using a script type in the Print Shop programs.

- A good way to emphasize a word within a block is to type it in capital letters. Variations on this theme: bold the word, underline the word, or use all three techniques together.

- Most text blocks you use in your project will look best if they are positioned in the center of the block space. If you're placing them around graphic blocks, positioning them at the top or bottom of the block space may help.

- Always preview the text by selecting Preview (PSD) or F10 (NPS) if you're unsure of your choices.

- Framing your text block is a good way to set it off for special attention, such as a date and time, or perhaps a price.

- Another way to draw attention to a block of text is to add a mini-border around it. There are many styles to choose from.

- Bazooka, Fillmore, Scribble, Standout, and Steamer fonts are available in uppercase letters only.

Grasping Your Graphics

One of the most remarkable features of the Print Shop programs is the interchangability of graphics. They allow you to create hundreds of different looks for each project.

This section will give you some more information on how to modify your graphics using the various editing options, provide other graphics options to consider, and offer tips to make your projects more professional-looking. Because the graphics are handled differently depending on what program you have, this section is divided into two parts; one part focuses on PSD graphics (DOS and Windows), the other on NPS graphics.

PSD Graphics—DOS and Windows

Remembering that any graphic is a piece of artwork you include in your project, you're all set to find out what to do with each type. As you learned in Section 1 of this book, there are three types of graphics in PSD: *square*, *row*, and *column*.

You'll find 96 square graphics (including tile patterns), 23 column graphics, and 25 row graphics to choose from. You'll find even more in the Calendar (26) and Initial Caps (11) files. There are also 114 backdrop graphics, including tall, wide, side and top spread, and banner backdrops. There are 35 borders, and 20 ruled lines. Plus, there are add-on graphics libraries you can purchase to expand your art selections even more. And if you have a previous version of a Print Shop program on your computer, you can use graphics from it as well. Obviously, you've got a lot of choices to make.

But even if this amount of graphics isn't enough, you can always modify or change the look of your art by using the editing commands. Editing commands are available from pull-down menus, or the tool palette in PSD-Windows. If you're using PSD-DOS, the editing commands appear when you select a graphic. Figure 5.1 shows the Edit box from PSD-DOS.

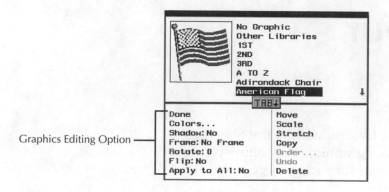

Figure 5.1
The graphic Edit box
from PSD, DOS
version.

Graphics Editing Option —

Editing PSD Graphics

Within the PSD-DOS Edit box or the PSD-Windows pull-down menus and Tool palette, you can choose colors, shadows, rotate, flip, stretch, and more. All these options can create different art looks. The following list details what each command does when you edit a graphic. (These same options are available on PSD-Windows from the pull-down menu bar or the Tool palette. You learned about the Tool palette in Section 1.)

Colors   This allows you to change color, shading, and background (Behind Text) of your graphic. For example, you can have a black graphic with a grey drop shadow on a yellow background by selecting the various color options. (See Figure 5.2.)

*Figure 5.2
An example of a
graphic with color
options controlled
by the Color
command.*

Shadow   Lets you place a shadow behind a graphic, looking as if the graphic has depth. See Figure 5.3 to see the difference between a plain graphic and one with a shadow.

*Figure 5.3
An example of a
graphic, with and
without a shadow.*

| **Frame** | Lets you put a box around the graphic. There are several styles to choose from: thin, thick, double line, or drop shadow. Figure 5.4 shows an example of a framed graphic. |

Figure 5.4
A framed graphic.

| **Rotate** | Allows you to tilt the graphic block in varying degrees. PSD-DOS users can specify the exact angle of rotation. PSD-Windows users can manually rotate the block with the Rotate tool from the tool palette, or specify exact degrees. In release 1.2, you can use negative numbers to rotate clockwise. |

Figure 5.5
A graphic rotated 25 degrees.

| **Flip** | You can flip a graphic horizontally or vertically, giving you a new perspective on your art. Figure 5.6 shows what a horizontally-flipped graphic looks like. |

Figure 5.6   A plain graphic on left, a horizontally flipped graphic on right.

| **Apply to All** | This allows you to apply your graphic edits to all graphic blocks of the same kind. For example, if your project has four square graphic blocks, you can apply the edits you make on the first block to all of the blocks, without having to select and modify each one separately. To use this command, select Yes, and any changes you make to the graphic from that point on will be made to other like graphics blocks as well. (Move, Scale, Stretch, Copy, Order, and Undo commands do not work with the Apply to All command. To turn these functions back on, select No.) |

Move	Lets you reposition the graphic block in the project.
Scale	Lets you reproportion the size of the graphic block, larger or smaller.
Stretch	Allows you to distort the shape of the block, squishing in or stretching out. You can create some very interesting looks by stretching or squishing your art. Take a look at Figure 5.7 to see what this command does.

*Figure 5.7
An example of
different looks
created by using the
Stretch command.*

Copy	This command duplicates the graphic block and lets you place the copy wherever you want.
Order	Lets you position, or layer, a block in the foreground or background of your project. This is useful for placing graphics underneath text and creating different layers of blocks (see Figure 5.8). However, the backdrop art is always considered the back layer of your project, and the border is always the front layer.

*Figure 5.8
Here are two
graphics that have
been layered over
each other to form a
new piece of art.*

Undo	Will undo your last command.
Delete	Wipes out your block completely.

If you're using PSD-DOS release 1.2, you'll find a new option in your Edit menu for backdrops—Page Blend. This new feature lets you blend the page color from one color to another. This is a special effect you can use with any of your Backdrops. It gives you six effects: solid, blend across, blend down, double blend, radiant blend, and diagonal blend. Try them all out to see what color effects you can achieve.

PSD-Windows Users   If you're working with PSD-Windows, you'll be using the pull-down menus from the Menu bar and the tools from the Tool palette to make your graphic edits. (See Section 1 for more information about the Tool palette.) In case you're having trouble locating all the editing commands just described, here's where to find them:

Colors	Tool palette.
Shadow	Object menu.
Frame	Tool palette or Object menu.
Rotate	Tool palette or Object menu. (To type in specific degrees, choose Rotate from the Object menu, then select Other.)
Flip	Tool palette or Object menu.
Apply to All	Called *Select All* on the Edit menu.
Move	Use the pointer tool from the Tool palette.
Scale	Object menu.
Stretch	Use the Pointer tool, click on a graphic corner, hold down the mouse button and move the mouse to stretch or squeeze a graphic block.
Copy	Edit menu.
Paste	Edit menu.
Order	Object menu.
Undo	Edit menu.
Delete	Tool palette or Edit menu.

More Graphics

In addition to the graphics you already know about, there are two more to learn: *initial caps* and *calendar graphics*. These square graphic types are available when you choose Other Libraries at the top of your graphic menu list. Initial caps can be found in the file *INITCAPS.PSG* (in Windows the file is called *PSDeluxe Initial Caps*). Calendar graphics are in a file called *CALENDAR.PSG* (in Windows the file is called *PSDeluxe Calendar Icons*). There are 11 initial caps graphics to choose from, and 26 calendar graphics.

Initial Caps

Initial caps are decorative boxes that you can use as backgrounds for single capital letters. See Figure 5.9 for an example. Initial caps graphics can be used for creating projects, such as a certificate, that require a more formal look. They can also be used for the first letter of the first sentence that starts out a fairy tale, or other documents that rely on a lot of text. Scaled large, they make nice backgrounds for blocks of text or a square graphic.

*Figure 5.9
An initial cap graphic with a text block layered on top.*

To use an initial cap, select the one you want from the menu list (make sure you're using *Other Libraries* and the initial caps file) and follow these steps:

1. Scale the graphic to the size you want.

2. Add a text or headline block on top of the initial cap background.

3. Type one letter in the block.

To continue a sentence, just add another text block beside the initial cap graphic.

Calendar Graphics

Calendar graphics are made for fitting in small spaces, like in a calendar. They're monochrome (black-and-white) graphics, but you can change them to colors. You'll find uses for them in many other PSD projects besides calendars.

To use, simply select the graphic you want from the calendar graphics file and scale it to fit, if necessary. See Figure 5.10 to see how a calendar graphic looks in a calendar project.

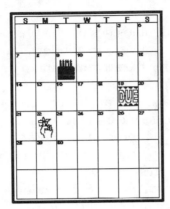

Figure 5.10
A calendar graphic
in place.

Borders, Mini Borders, and Ruled Lines

The decorative borders and ruled lines can further your graphic potential when you're creating projects. A border or ruled line can give your project a distinct look, and a mini-border can draw attention to an important text or graphic block. Ruled lines can add some punch between text blocks. There's only one thing to remember about borders, mini-borders, and ruled lines. Borders cannot be moved, scaled, or stretched. However, mini-borders can be. Both mini-borders and ruled lines can be modified with editing commands. Knowing that, you can experiment with mini-borders and ruled lines to fashion a variety of graphic effects.

The Graphics Exporter

You can use the Graphics Exporter to export your PSD graphics into other programs, with the exception of banner backdrops, borders and mini-borders, and ruled lines. When you installed PSD, the Graphics Exporter was automatically installed. You must close your PSD program and return to the DOS prompt to use the Graphics Exporter.

If you're using PSD-DOS, type Export and press Enter to start. Choose "Select a Graphics Library" from the Main menu and press Enter. Choose your desired library, the exact graphic, and the file format you wish to use. Also select a destination for your exported graphic—where is it going? When finished with selections, press Enter to export. Select "Exit to DOS" to return to the DOS prompt.

If you're using PSD-Windows, just double-click on the Graphics Exporter icon in the PSD Program group window. Choose the graphics library that contains the art you want to export. Then choose the particular graphic to be exported. Next, pick what kind of file format from the list of available choices. (This depends on how you're going to use the graphic, what program you're going to put it into, etc.) If prompted, choose a size. Finally, choose a destination for your graphic file. Once that's done, you can exit the utility by pressing Escape. For more information about the utility, consult your PSD-Windows manual. Now you can go into the program into which you exported your graphic.

Importing Graphics from Other Programs

Good news for PSD-Windows, you can import graphics from other programs! You can import two kinds of other graphics: those created in an older version of NPS, or those made using Windows bitmaps (BMP format), such as the Windows Paintbrush program or any other program that makes BMP files. The easiest way to place a graphic that has been created in another program is to use the Windows Clipboard. The Clipboard is a temporary storage space. Within the program the art originates from, copy the art to the Clipboard by using the Copy command from the Edit menu. Move to the PSD-Windows program and open the project file into which you want to import the art, simply select Paste from the Edit menu, and place your imported art into your project.

If you're a PSD-DOS user, you cannot import other graphics—unless you have PSD release 1.2. This latest release does allow you to bring in new art (EPS, PCX, TIFF files) from other drawing programs.

To import a graphic, just select Add New Elements, Imported Graphics, the desired file format, and the exact graphic location and art piece. Once imported, you can move, scale, frame, and more.

PSD-Windows Extras

If you're using the Windows version of PSD, you'll find a few extra editing commands at your fingertips. On the Object menu, there is a command for locking or unlocking your blocks. That's to keep them from being accidentally moved. When selected, this command will lock your block into place so that it cannot be moved, rotated, flipped, scaled, stretched, resized, ordered, or deleted.

Also on the Object menu is a command for aligning blocks. This editing technique is good to use when "eyeballing" a block into place is too difficult. Select Align and choose the alignment you want from the dialog box. There are 11 alignment options to choose from.

The View menu offers you a chance to see different perspectives of your project. You can zoom in for a closer look, zoom out, see the project at actual size, or various percentages of the actual size. Also on the View menu are options for hiding the backdrop, or the Tool palette. These options also expand on your viewing perspectives.

NPS Graphics

NPS graphics vary from those used in the PSD programs. You can choose from 5 wide borders, 10 thin borders, 37 square graphics, 10 full panel graphics, and 3 graphic patterns. You can also modify your graphics in the Customize menu, shown in Figure 5.11. This menu selection becomes available after you've started building a project. Just select Customize from the menu list. You can enlarge, reduce, flip, change colors, add shadows, and more.

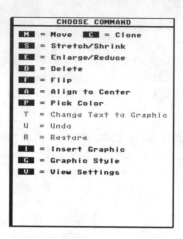

Figure 5.11
The Customize menu from NPS.

The highlighted letters in Figure 5.11 must be pressed to select an editing command. Unavailable choices will appear dim. The Customize menu is the same for both text editing and graphic editing. If you're editing text, only five editing options are turned on. If you're editing art, almost all the options are available. The following list describes the different editing functions avaiable.

Move	Lets you move the block to another location. Use the arrow keys to move the block, press Enter when finished.
Clone	Lets you copy a block (useful in creating symmetry in your project). Use the arrow keys to move the duplicate block to a new position.
Stretch/ Shrink	Lets you scale a block, such as making it elongated. Use the arrow keys to shrink or stretch a block, and press Enter when finished.
Enlarge/ Reduce	Lets you resize a block proportionately. Use with the plus and minus keys on the numeric keypad. Press Enter when the size is how you want it.
Delete	Erases a block.

Flip	Lets you flip a block horizontally or vertically. After selecting this command, press the H key to flip horizontally, or the V key to flip vertically.
Align to Center	Lets you align the block within the project. Press H to align horizontally, V to align vertically, or B to align a block both ways.
Pick Color	Allows you to choose a color for the block components or background.
Change Text to Graphic	Allows the system to treat a text block just like a graphics block.
Undo	Undoes your last action (except for Change Text to Graphic).
Restore	Restores the earlier version of your project if you saved it before going into the Customize menu.
Insert Graphic	Lets you put another graphic block in. Once the new graphic has been determined, use the arrow keys to position it and press Enter.
Graphic Style	Lets you make special effects to graphics blocks similar to those available for text blocks. *Standard* is a regular graphic. *Solid* will create an outline of space around the graphic if it overlaps another block. *Outline* will outline the graphic. *Raised* gives the graphic a feeling of depth, as if it's been embossed. *3-D* gives your graphic a 3-dimensional look. *Shadow* creates a shadow effect around the graphic.
View Settings	Tells you what choices have been made for that block so far. For example, color, position, etc.

The New Print Shop Graphic Editor

Here's a Print Shop feature that the PSD programs don't have. The NPS *Graphic Editor* lets you change graphics physically, or draw new ones. You can take an existing graphic and personalize it to look the way you want. Or you can start from scratch and draw your own square graphic to use in projects.

To use this feature, select Graphic Editor from the Main menu screen. Figure 5.12 shows what the Graphic Editor screen looks like.

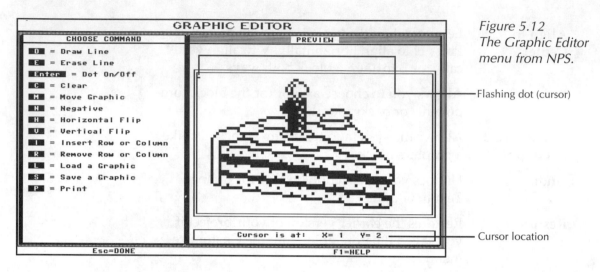

Figure 5.12
The Graphic Editor menu from NPS.

Flashing dot (cursor)

Cursor location

A small, flashing dot will appear in the upper left corner of the preview window. That's the *drawing cursor*. It can be moved with the arrow keys. The Graphic Editor is set up like a grid. Each space you move with an arrow key is a point on that grid. As you are drawing, the box at the bottom of the preview window will show you your coordinates on the grid. The horizontal position on the grid is called the *x-coordinate*, or *x-axis*. The vertical position is called the *y-coordinate*, or *y-axis*.

Needless to say, the size of this grid and the little cursor you will draw with is sure to cause some strain on your eyes! But if you're bound and determined to draw your own graphics, the following list will describe the menu commands to use.

Draw Line   Select this command to draw on your graphic. Each spot drawn on the grid is a dot. As the dots connect, they become lines. When you've positioned the cursor where you want the drawing to start, press D. Then use the arrow keys to move the line as you draw. Press the Spacebar to change color intensity (dark to light) of the line. Press Enter when you've finished.

Erase Line   Choosing this command turns your cursor into an eraser. Use this technique to delete lines you don't want. Every time you move the arrow, the cursor will erase the line beneath it.

Dot On/Off Works the same as pressing the Spacebar: it changes the color intensity of the dot from light to dark.

Clear Deletes everything in the preview window.

Move Graphic Lets you move the graphic around the space with the arrow keys. But if you move any part of the graphic outside the edges of the window, it's gone forever!

Negative Changes all the light dots to dark, and all the dark dots to light. Blank areas also become dark.

Horizontal Flip Allows you to flip everything in the preview window horizontally.

Vertical Flip Allows you to flip a graphic vertically.

Insert Row or Column Lets you insert a blank row or column wherever your cursor is positioned. However, when you use this command, a row or column at the bottom of the preview window is deleted to make room for your insertion.

Remove Row or Column Lets you erase an entire row or column at wherever your cursor is positioned. However, when you use this command, a row or column at the bottom of the preview window is added.

Load a Graphic Lets you work with an existing graphic. You can make changes and save it as a new graphic.

Save a Graphic Allows you to save the graphic you've created or modified on the Graphic Editor. You can name the new (or altered) graphic, and use it later in a project.

Print Will give you a printout of the graphic. It will be the size of a small graphic.

Exit To end your work in the Graphic Editor, press Esc to exit.

PSD and NPS Graphics Tips

The following is a list of tips to apply when working with graphics in your projects.

- You can take ruled lines, column graphics, or row graphics and rotate them to create new borders or frames. (PSD-DOS and Windows.)

- Too much artwork will make your project too busy, and your message might get lost! Don't feel like you have to put a piece of artwork into every blank space. A good theory to follow is: "less is more."

- Many of the graphics work well layered together. Use the Order command to experiment with this kind of effect.

- Graphics make great screened backdrops to your projects. *Screened backdrops* appear as lightened art behind text or other objects. To turn a graphic into a screened backdrop, edit the graphic, select colors, and lighten the color shade. But be careful when you place text over a screened backdrop. Make sure the text is bold enough and large enough to stand out from the shaded background.

- Experiment with graphics that appear half on and half off your project page. This creates some interesting looks.

- Ruled lines combined with square graphics can create very contemporary looks. Experiment with combining both of these graphics types for a "modern art" style.

- If you don't have a color printer, don't forget about adding color after a project is printed. Markers, colored pencils, and paint are great ways to spiff up your artwork.

- Many of the square graphics make wonderful logos for businesses, especially when modified to your tastes. Logos are perfect for any correspondence: letterhead, business cards, envelopes, etc.

Installation Instructions

If you've not yet installed your Print Shop program yet, follow these handy instructions:

Installing PSD for DOS:

1. Insert PSD Disk 1 into drive A. (If you're using a different drive, insert the disk into that drive, and substitute that drive letter for A in the following instructions.) Type A: and press Enter. (If you have Windows on your computer, you must exit Windows to install PSD.)

2. At theDOS prompt, type **Install** and press Enter. An introduction screen will appear, detailing how the installation program works. Press Enter and the installation screen will appear.

3. Select Install Print Shop Deluxe by pressing Enter. (Or click the left mouse button.) A screen will appear, asking you to enter a name. Type your name and press Enter. You can type in a second name, company, or school name on the second line, and press Enter afterward. Press Enter again to confirm. (If you made a mistake, use the arrow keys to go back to the line and edit. Press Enter to continue.)

4. The next instruction will ask you to enter the disk drive and the directory on which you want to install your program. If you do not specify a drive or directory, the program will install the copy on the C drive, in a directory named PSDELUXE. Press Enter to continue.

5. Now the program will install itself. Follow the on-screen instructions to insert each disk.

6. Another screen will appear, asking if you want to install one of the fonts. If so, select Install all the fonts by pressing Enter (or by clicking with the left mouse button).

7. When the program has been installed, you will be returned to the installation screen. Select Exit Install and press Enter to leave the installation program.

Appendix A

Installing Release 1.2   If you're installing PSD release 1.2, the installation screen in Step 3 will give you four choices. Choose "Install The Print Shop Deluxe" by pressing Enter to install the program. If you have an earlier version of PSD on your computer, you will be asked if you would like to install over that version. If you say yes, your earlier project files will be saved. All fonts are automatically installed in release 1.2 installation.

Installing a Graphics Collection or Folio   Follow the same steps as listed, but choose "Install Graphics Collection" (or "Install Add-on Graphics Collection" if you're using release 1.2 to install a collection, or "Install Add-on Graphics Folio" to install a graphics folio) at the installation screen.

Installing PSD for Windows

1. Starting from the Program Manager screen of your Windows program, insert Print Shop Deluxe Disk 1 into drive A. (If you're using a different drive, insert the disk into that drive, and substitute that drive letter for A in the following instructions.)

2. Pull down the File menu from the menu bar, and select Run.

3. Type **a:setup** in the Command Line box. Click on OK.

4. Enter the name of the disk drive and directory on which you want to install your program. If you do not specify a drive or directory, the program will install the copy on the C drive, in a directory named PSDWIN. Press Enter to continue.

5. Now the program will install itself. Follow the on-screen instructions to insert each disk.

6. When the installation procedure is complete, you'll be returned to the Program Manager window.

Installing NPS

1. Starting at the DOS prompt, change to your A drive by typing **a:** and pressing Enter.

2. Insert The Print Shop Program disk into drive A.

3. At the DOS prompt, type **Install**. Press the Enter key.

4. Instructions will appear on-screen, telling you how to proceed. First select the *default setting* (the one with an asterisk) by pressing Enter. (If you'd like to choose another option, type the number of the option.)

5. Select the disk drive and directory on which you want to install the program. NEWPS is the default name.

6. When the installation procedure is complete, you're ready to go.

Program Tip Don't forget to make backup copies of your disks and keep them in a safe place.

Appendix A

A Word About the Add-On Libraries

As if there weren't enough projects to build with your Print Shop program version, you can purchase additional graphics libraries that instantly increase the amount of art available. The choices become almost mind-boggling!

For example, Print Shop Deluxe, for both DOS and Windows, offers more graphics collections to add to your capabilities, such as Print Shop Deluxe Sampler Graphics Collection or Print Shop Deluxe Business Graphics Collections. The PSD Sampler Graphics Collection will add 29 backdrops, 10 banner backdrops, 14 tiled pattern and 32 square graphics, 16 row graphics, 13 column graphics, 25 borders, and 20 ruled lines to your current PSD program. Additional graphics, like the Print Shop Deluxe Comic Characters Collection, with 320 comic art pieces, can offer you tons of art to choose from. And there are sure to be more collections available in the future, so keep your eye out! (See the PSD coupon at the end of this book for more!)

If you're using NPS, you'll find additional fonts and art available in The New Print Shop Graphics Library Editions, such as the Sampler Edition, the Party Edition, and the School & Business Edition. Each collection offers 10 more fonts, 50 small graphics, 5 patterns, 13 full panel graphics, 5 banner graphics, 2 letterhead graphics, and 5 thin borders.

You'll also find more uses for your NPS program's capabilities with The New Print Shop Companion. This add-on program offers you the ability to type letters, envelopes, reports, and newsletters right on your screen. It also has a Graphic Importer feature that allows you to bring in art from other programs to use in your Print Shop programs. You can use the Editors to modify art, fonts, and borders to create your own styles. You'll also find a Cataloger to help you organize and keep track of all your project files.

Appendix B

You'll want to expand your program with these add-on libraries—they'll give you even more project designs to choose from. To see a catalog of all the art available on the PSD (DOS and Windows) program, see Appendix C.

Print Shop Deluxe Fonts

BAZOOKA
Boulder
Calligrapher
Chaucer
FILLMORE
Heather
Jester
Librarian
Moderne
NewZurica
NewZurica Bold
NewZurica Oblique
Palatia
Palatia Bold
Palatia Italic

Paramount
Paramount Bold
Paramount Italic
SCRIBBLE
Sherwood
Signature
StageCoach
STANDOUT
STEAMER
Stylus
Subway
Tribune
Tribune Bold
Tribune Italic
Tubular

Print Shop Deluxe Graphics

Square Graphics

1st

Adirondack
Chair

2nd

American Flag

3rd

Apple
Basket

A to Z

Baseball

Basketball

Bunny

Children

Biblical Angel

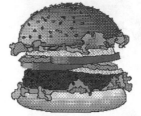

Burger

Cruise Ship

Birthday Cake

Candy Cane

Deco Element

Birthday Hippo

Celtic Cross

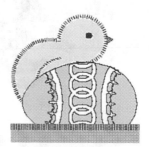

Egg & Chick

Birthday Icon

Cherry Pie

Elephant Forgets

*Father
Time*

Graduation

Ink & Pen

Firecracker

*Happy
Tooth*

International No

*Floppy
Disk 3.5*

Hockey

*Kid &
Baseball*

*Floppy
Disk 5.25*

*Holiday
Stamp*

Knowledge

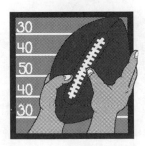
Football

Holly

Leprechaun

Appendix D

Lily Ornament

Menorah

Owl

Lizards

Music

Paintbrush

Lovable Pup

New Year's Baby

Party Couple

Lunch

No Smoking

Pets

Math

Ornament

Pumpkin

Pushpin

Sale

Starfish

Red Cross

Soccer

Stork & Bundle

Restaurant Icon

Spaceship

Swans

Running

Speech Bubble

Teddy

Running Computer

Star of David

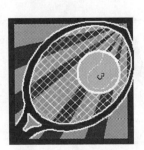
Tennis

Appendix D

Thought Bubble

Volleyball

World

Torah

Wildflowers

Square Graphic Patterns

Tropical Drinks

Wine & Bread

ABC's

Valentine

Witch & Moon

Balloons

Victorian Biker

Woman in Hat

Bats & Pumpkins

*Cake
Slices*

Gifts

*Red
Balloons*

Christmas Trees

Leaves & Acorns

Star of David

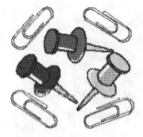

*Clips &
Tacks*

Lips! Lips!

*Three-D
Shapes*

Cross

New Year

Turkey

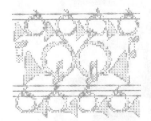

French Horns

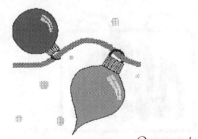

Ornaments

Appendix D

Appendix D　**221**

Calendar Graphics

Briefcase

Due

Athletic Shoes

Car Trip

Exclamation

Balloon

Child Playing

Flag

Birthday Cake

Cityscape

Heart

Book

Closed

House

Lunch

Music

Television

Mail

Phone

Ticket

Medical Symbol

Plane

Initial Cap
Square
Graphics

Meeting

Reminder

Border
& Stars

Money

Sunny Day

Decor

Appendix D

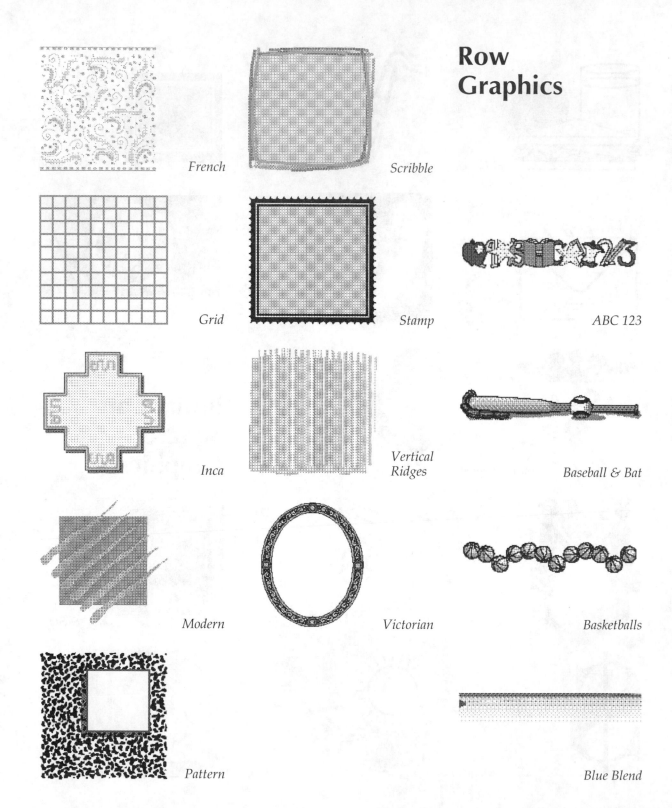

Row
Graphics

French

Scribble

Grid

Stamp

ABC 123

Inca

Vertical Ridges

Baseball & Bat

Modern

Victorian

Basketballs

Pattern

Blue Blend

Chickens

Haunted Cemetery

Music

Cupids

Ink Swash

Nativity

Cups & String

Jolly Pumpkins

Noah's Ark

Dreidels

Jukebox

Orange Slices

Football Players

Memo

Parade

Appendix D

Column
Graphics

Party Snake

Shell

Easter Lilies

Snowman & Hearth

Balloons

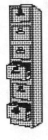

File Cabinet

Today's Special

Today's Special

Bat & Gloves

Football Player

Halloween Candy

Herbs

Lipstick

Hearts

Lightning Bolt

Memo Pencil

Appendix D

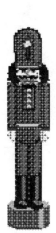

Mod Cafe Cups

Pen

Pillar

Nutcracker

Penguin

Presents

Restaurant Table

Space Ships

Waiter

Southwest Strip

Tulip Ornament

Walking Man

Appendix D

Backdrops

Tall (Portrait) Backdrops

Coastal Scene

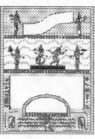
Egyptian Party

Baby Animals

Column & Pen

Football Field

Baby Quilt

Confetti

Fruit & Leaves

Bon Voyage

Diner Food

Geometric Fax

Clown & Hoop

Easter Basket

Gingerbread Man

 *Gradient Cone*

 *Mod Cafe*

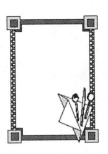 *Sand Castle*

 *Haunted House*

 *Notebook*

 *Shamrocks & Hat*

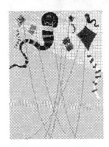 *Kites*

 *Ocean & Jungle*

 *Sheep in Field*

 *Lilies & Birds*

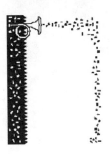 *Party Trumpet*

 *UFO*

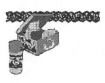 *Lunch Box*

 *Potpourri*

 *Valentine Hearts*

Appendix D

Volcano

Celtic

Fireworks

Winter Child

Clown & Confetti

Goofy Stork

Winter Snowscape

Cornflowers

Haunted Tree

Woodpecker

Cupcakes & Candy

Party Horn

Top Fold Spread Backdrops

Butterfly

Doves & Mint

Watch & Confetti

Wet Duck

Wide (Landscape) Backdrops

Clown with Card

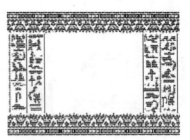

Egyptian

American Flag

Crab on Beach

Football Collage

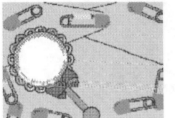

Baby Things

Dance Party

Kids

Butterflies

Dino Birthday

Party Invitation

Candy Box

Dragon

Recipe Card

Appendix D

Side Fold Spread Backdrops

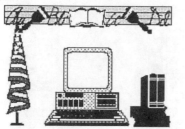

Schoolroom

Tropical Palms

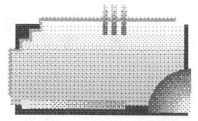

Gradient

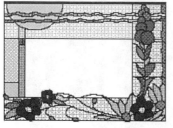

Stained Glass

Birthday Cow

Graduation Caps

Summer Sea

Birthday Mice

Harvest Maize

Three Wise Men

Christmas Sleigh

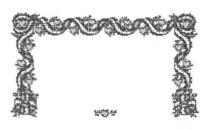

Hearts & Ribbon

Tree & Presents

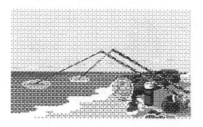

Fishing

Hourglass

Paper Clown

Sleeping Bunny

Travel

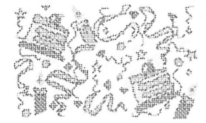

Pastel Birthday

Southwest

Witch & Spider

Banner Backdrops

Horizontal

Art Deco

Balloons

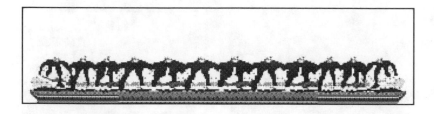

Banana Split

Celebration

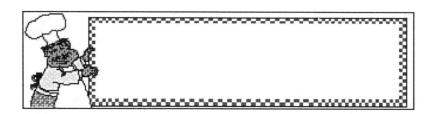

Chef

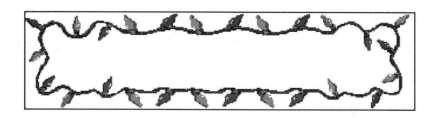

Christmas Lights

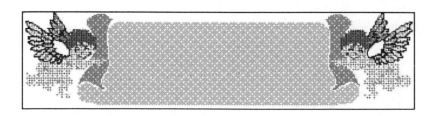

Cupids

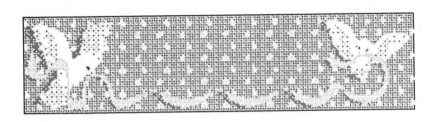

Doves & Ribbon

Elephants

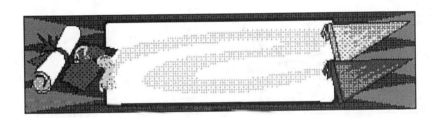

Grad Pennant

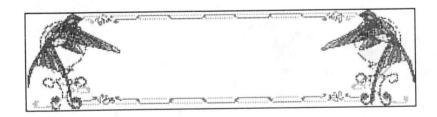

Nouveau Birds

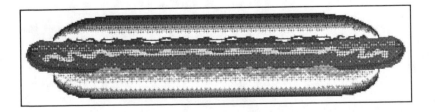

Hot Dog

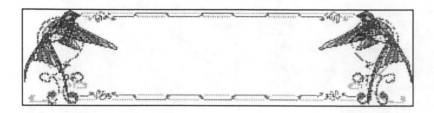

Nouveau Bird

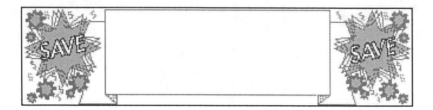

Save

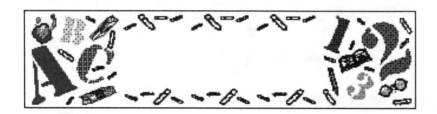

School Jumble

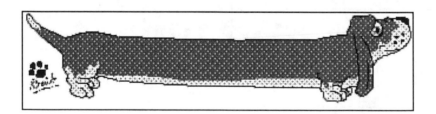

Stretch Dog

Vertical

Christmas Town

Doggone Birthday

Ice Cream Cone

Kid Pyramid

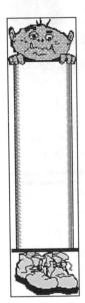
Ogre

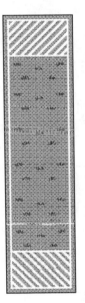
Playing Field

Appendix D

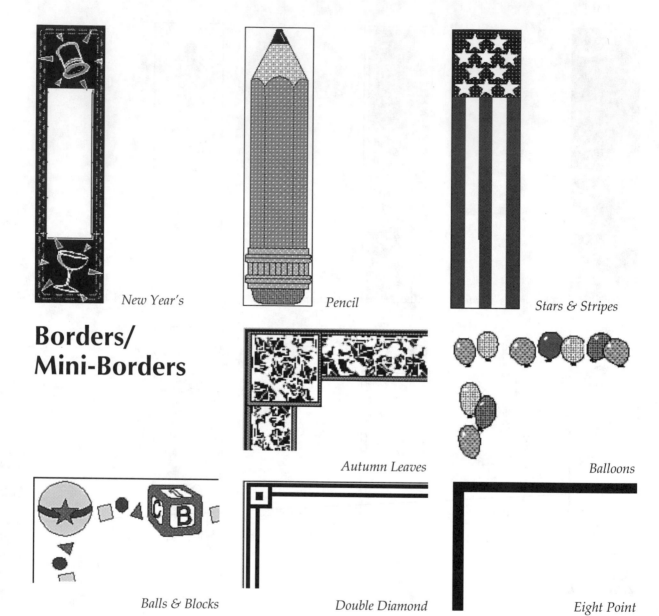

New Year's

Pencil

Stars & Stripes

Borders/ Mini-Borders

Autumn Leaves

Balloons

Balls & Blocks

Double Diamond

Eight Point

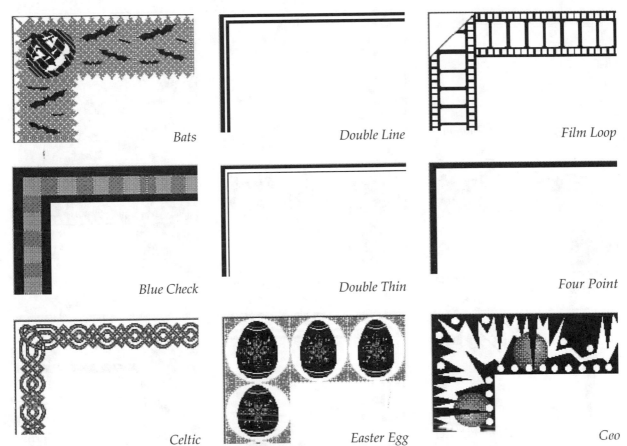

Bats

Double Line

Film Loop

Blue Check

Double Thin

Four Point

Celtic

Easter Egg

Ceo

Diamond Corners

Egyptian

Joined Lines

Appendix D

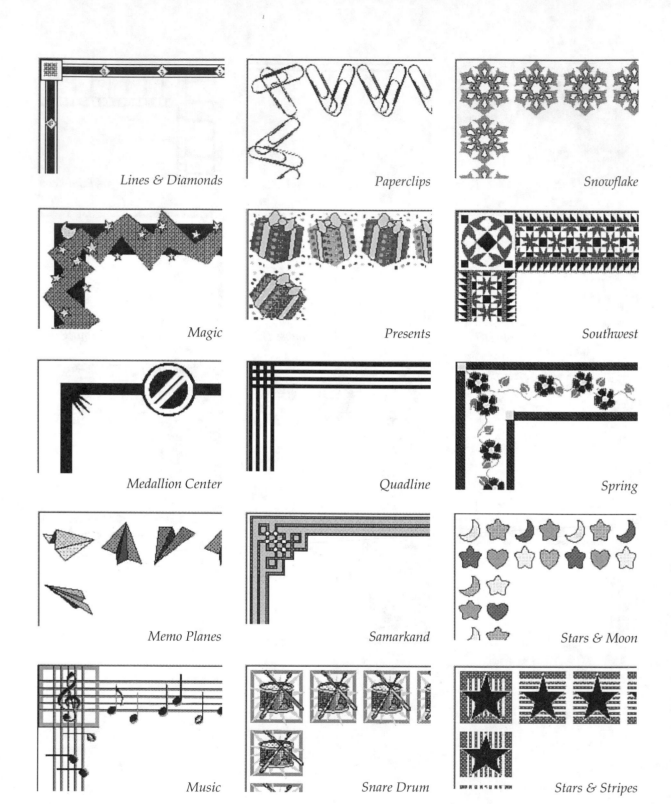

Lines & Diamonds

Paperclips

Snowflake

Magic

Presents

Southwest

Medallion Center

Quadline

Spring

Memo Planes

Samarkand

Stars & Moon

Music

Snare Drum

Stars & Stripes

Ruled Lines

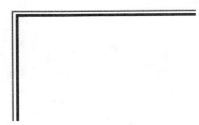

Thick Border

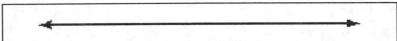

Arrow

Thin Border

Baby Pins

Triangle

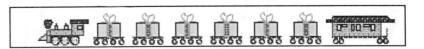

Birthday Train

Cactus

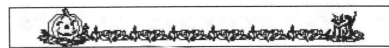

Cat & Pumpkin

Appendix D

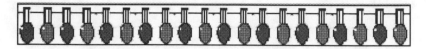

Christmas Lights

Circus Trim

Easter Eggs

Elephants

Flower Vine

Grape Vines

Leaves & Ribbon

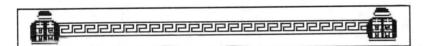

Oriental Pot

Paper Links

Sampler Stitch

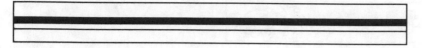

Scotch

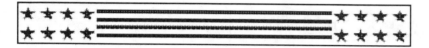

Stars & Stripes

Traditional

Wedding Lace

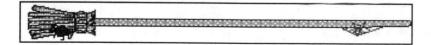

Witch's Broom

Index

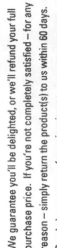